The Carb Cornucopia: 97 Delicious Variations of the Classic Pasta Dish

Savory Delights Akan

Contents

INTRODUCTION

The Carbonara Cornucopia: 97 Delicious Variations of the Classic Pasta Dish is a cookbook every pasta lover must have. Pasta is a staple food in almost every household around the world. Amongst the numerous pasta dishes, Carbonara pasta is one of the most popular. Carbonara pasta is a classic Italian dish that has been enjoyed for generations. It is made by tossing hot spaghetti with a creamy, cheesy, and salty sauce of eggs, pancetta or bacon, and Parmesan cheese.

The Carbonara Cornucopia is a collection of Carbonara recipes that will surprise and delight any food lover. The cookbook features 97 unique variations of the classic Carbonara pasta dish. It is an ultimate collection of Carbonara recipes that will surely excite anyone who is tired of the traditional Carbonara recipe.

The book explores the versatility of Carbonara pasta by adding various ingredients to the dish, making it more flavorful and exciting. The cookbook features Carbonara recipes that use different types of pasta, such as fettuccine, linguine, and penne. It also has recipes that incorporate vegetables, such as mushrooms, asparagus, and spinach into the mix. The cookbook even includes Carbonara recipes that utilize seafood, such as salmon, shrimp, and scallops.

The Carbonara Cornucopia is a cookbook that will enable anyone to create a unique Carbonara pasta dish, showcasing their creativity in the kitchen. The cookbook is filled with easy-to-follow instructions and photographs that will guide anyone to make a delicious Carbonara dish. The book is written in a simple language that makes even beginners in the kitchen comfortable enough to try new recipes.

The Carbonara Cornucopia is more than just a collection of Carbonara pasta recipes; it is a celebration of Italy's culinary heritage. It is a tribute to the Italian culture by showcasing one of their most beloved pasta dishes in unique ways. The cookbook invites you on a journey to explore different flavors and textures, merging timeless Carbonara pasta with various ingredients, creating a new level of flavor.

The Carbonara Cornucopia is ideal for anyone seeking to diversify their pasta recipes or those who want to impress their family and guests with a new and exciting Carbonara dish. The cookbook is perfect for pasta lovers who crave flavor and a twist to classic recipes. As a cookbook that will enable anyone to explore their creativity and experiment with ingredients, The Carbonara Cornucopia is a must-have.

In conclusion, The Carbonara Cornucopia is an ultimate cookbook that provides 97 unique variations of Carbonara pasta, taking the popular Italian dish to another level. The cookbook is an exploration of the versatility of the Carbonara pasta recipe, infused with various ingredients that will awaken your taste buds. With easy-to-follow instructions and photographs, the cookbook is perfect for anyone who loves to cook or wants to explore the world of pasta. Get a copy today and join the journey of creating flavorful and exciting Carbonara dishes.

1. Classic Pasta Carbonara

Classic Pasta Carbonara is a classic Italian dish of spaghetti pasta, bacon, eggs, cream, and cheese. Rich, delicious, and ready quickly, this dish is a delight for many pasta lovers.

Serving: 4
Preparation Time: 10 minutes
Ready Time: 20 minutes

Ingredients:
- 8 ounces of spaghetti pasta
- 4 slices bacon
- 2 eggs
- 1/3 cup heavy cream
- 1/4 cup Parmesan cheese, grated
- Salt and black pepper, to taste

Instructions:
1. Boil a large pot of salted water over high heat. Once boiling, add the spaghetti pasta and cook according to the manufacturer's Instructions or until al dente.
2. Meanwhile, place a large skillet over medium heat. Add the bacon and cook until crisp. Using a slotted spoon, remove the bacon from the skillet and place it on a plate lined with paper towels. Set aside.
3. In a medium bowl, whisk together the eggs, cream, Parmesan cheese, and generous amounts of salt and freshly ground black pepper.
4. To the bacon fat in the skillet, add the cooked spaghetti pasta and stir to combine. Reduce the heat to low and add the egg and cream mixture, stirring everything together until the eggs are cooked through.
5. Serve the pasta garnished with the cooked bacon, more Parmesan cheese, and freshly ground black pepper. Enjoy!

Nutrition Information: Per serving: 408 calories, 30 g fat, 14 g saturated fat, 43 g carbohydrates, 9 g protein, 2 g fiber, 1290 mg sodium.

2. Vegetarian Carbonara

Vegetarian Carbonara is a creamy and flavorful Italian-style pasta dish made with plant-based Ingredients. It is a perfect meatless main that's on the table in under 30 minutes.
Serving: 4
Preparation Time: 10 minutes
Ready Time: 20 minutes

Ingredients:
- 1 pound spaghetti
- 2 tablespoons olive oil
- 2 cloves garlic, minced
- 2 cups mushrooms, sliced
- 2 tablespoons vegan butter
- 2 tablespoons all-purpose flour
- 1 cup vegan cream
- 1 cup nutritional yeast
- 1 teaspoon sea salt
- 1/2 teaspoon black pepper
- 1/2 teaspoon cayenne
- 2 tablespoons vegan bacon bits
- 2 tablespoons chopped parsley

Instructions:
1. Bring a large pot of salted water to a boil. Cook spaghetti according to package Instructions. Drain and set aside.
2. Heat the olive oil in a large skillet over medium heat. Add the garlic, mushrooms, and vegan butter. Cook, stirring occasionally, until the mushrooms are softened and the butter is melted, about 5 minutes.
3. Reduce heat to low and sprinkle the flour on top. Stir for 1 minute then pour in the vegan cream, nutritional yeast, salt, pepper, and cayenne. Stir until the sauce thickens, about 5 minutes.
4. Add the cooked spaghetti to the skillet along with the bacon bits. Stir until everything is combined and the spaghetti is coated in the sauce.
5. Serve hot sprinkled with parsley.

Nutrition Information:

Calories: 365; Total Fat: 14.4 g; Saturated Fat: 4.5 g; Protein: 17.6 g; Total Carbohydrates: 45.3 g; Sodium: 569.1 mg; Cholesterol: 11.7 mg; Sugars: 4.6 g.

3. Chicken Carbonara

Chicken Carbonara is an Italian dish made with carbonara sauce, which is typically made with eggs, cheese, and bacon. This hearty meal is sure to be a hit at your next dinner gathering.
Serving: 6
Preparation Time: 15 minutes
Ready Time: 30 minutes

Ingredients:
- 2 tablespoons olive oil
- 2 skinless boneless chicken breasts, cut into 1/2-inch cubes
- 2 cloves garlic, minced
- 1/4 cup white onion, minced
- 6 slices bacon, cooked and crumbled
- 2 tablespoons white wine
- 1/4 cup heavy cream
- 2 tablespoons Parmesan cheese
- 2 tablespoons parsley, chopped
- 2 tablespoons butter
- Salt and pepper to taste

Instructions:
1. Heat the olive oil in a large skillet over medium heat. Add the chicken cubes and cook, stirring frequently, until the chicken is cooked through.
2. Add garlic and onion and cook for 2 minutes. Add bacon, white wine, and cream and bring to a simmer.
3. Reduce heat and add Parmesan cheese, parsley, butter, salt and pepper. Simmer for 5 minutes.
4. Serve over cooked pasta.

Nutrition Information:

Per Serving: Calories 269, Total Fat 18 g, Saturated Fat 8 g, Cholesterol 85 mg, Sodium 414 mg, Total Carbohydrates 3 g, Dietary Fiber 0 g, Sugars 0 g, Protein 19 g

4. Shrimp Carbonara

Shrimp Carbonara is a delicious Italian-inspired dish with an irresistible creamy cheese sauce. This simple one-dish recipe is an easy weeknight dinner.
Serving: 4
Preparation Time: 10 minutes
Ready Time: 20 minutes

Ingredients:
- 8 ounces penne pasta
- 1 tablespoon olive oil
- 6 ounces cooked and peeled shrimp
- 1/3 cup grated Parmesan cheese
- 2 cloves garlic, minced
- 1/4 cup white wine
- 1/2 cup heavy cream
- 2 tablespoons chopped fresh parsley
- Salt and pepper to taste

Instructions:
1. Bring a large pot of lightly salted water to a boil. Add the penne pasta and cook until al dente, about 8 minutes. Drain.
2. Heat the olive oil in a large skillet over medium heat. Add the shrimp and garlic, and cook for 2 minutes. Add the white wine, and cook for another 2 minutes.
3. Add the cream and Parmesan cheese, and bring to a simmer. Cook for about 5 minutes.
4. Add the cooked pasta and parsley, and stir to combine. Salt and pepper to taste.

Nutrition Information:
Calories: 373, Fat: 12g, Saturated Fat: 6g, Cholesterol: 133mg, Sodium: 363mg, Carbohydrates: 37g, Fiber: 2g, Sugar: 2g, Protein: 24g

5. Spaghetti Carbonara

Spaghetti Carbonara is an Italian pasta dish made with spaghetti, beaten eggs, butter, black pepper, and Parmesan cheese.
Serving: 6
Preparation time: 10 minutes
Ready time: 20 minutes

Ingredients:
- 500g spaghetti
- 6 large eggs
- 150g butter, diced
- Grated Parmesan cheese
- Coarse black pepper

Instructions:
1. Bring a large pot of salted water to a boil for the spaghetti.
2. Melt the butter over low heat in a large skillet.
3. In a large bowl, mix together the eggs, Parmesan cheese, and black pepper.
4. Once the water boils, add the spaghetti and cook for 10 minutes, stirring occasionally, until al dente.
5. Drain the spaghetti and add it to the melted butter. Stir over low heat for a minute to coat the spaghetti.
6. Remove the skillet from the heat and add the egg mixture. Stir quickly with a wooden spoon to coat the spaghetti.
7. Serve the spaghetti carbonara immediately with additional Parmesan cheese, if desired.

Nutrition Information:
Calories: 386 kcal, Carbohydrates: 33 g, Protein: 16 g, Fat: 20 g, Saturated Fat: 11 g, Cholesterol: 219 mg, Sodium: 185 mg, Potassium: 210 mg, Fiber: 2 g, Sugar: 1 g, Vitamin A: 617 IU, Vitamin C: 1 mg, Calcium: 158 mg, Iron: 2 mg.

6. Linguine Carbonara

Linguine Carbonara is a classic Italian dish that is both hearty and satisfying. The creamy sauce has a rich flavor that will have you reminiscing about the old country. In this recipe, we combine the deep flavor of classic bacon with the sweet notes of cream and parmesan for a real treat.
Serving: 4
Preparation Time: 15 minutes
Ready Time: 25 minutes

Ingredients:
- 4 ounces uncooked linguine
- 4 tablespoons butter
- 4 ounces diced pancetta
- 1/2 teaspoon garlic powder
- 1/2 cup heavy cream
- 2 tablespoons shredded parmesan
- 2 tablespoons fresh chopped parsley

Instructions:
1. Bring a large pot of salted water to a boil over medium-high heat.
2. Add the linguine and cook until al dente, about 7 minutes.
3. Drain and set aside.
4. In a large skillet, melt the butter over medium heat.
5. Add the pancetta and sauté for 3-4 minutes.
6. Add the garlic powder and stir in the heavy cream.
7. Simmer until the sauce has thickened, about 2 minutes.
8. Remove from the heat and add the parmesan and parsley.
9. Add the reserved linguine and toss to combine.
10. Serve immediately.

Nutrition Information:
Per Serving: Calories: 382, Fat: 23 g, Sodium: 279 mg, Carbohydrate: 30 g, Protein: 12 g

7. Rigatoni Carbonara

Rigatoni Carbonara is a classic Italian dish that combines handmade rigatoni pasta with a rich, creamy sauce of bacon, eggs, Parmesan cheese, and black pepper. This dish is simple and bursting with flavor.
Servings: 4
Preparation Time: 10 minutes
Ready Time: 25 minutes

Ingredients:
- 1 (16-ounce) package of rigatoni pasta
- 8 slices of bacon
- 2 large eggs, lightly beaten
- 1/2 cup grated Parmesan cheese
- Salt to taste
- Ground black pepper to taste

Instructions:
1. Bring a large pot of water to boil and cook the rigatoni al dente according to package Instructions.
2. While the pasta is cooking, in a large skillet over medium heat, add the bacon and cook until crisp. Once cooked, remove the bacon from the skillet and let drain on a paper towel-lined plate.
3. Reduce the heat to low and add the eggs to the pan, stirring constantly until the eggs are just cooked through, about 1-2 minutes.
4. Drain the pasta and return to pot. Stir in the egg mixture, Parmesan cheese, bacon, salt, and pepper.
5. Serve the rigatoni carbonara with extra Parmesan cheese and pepper, if desired. Enjoy!

Nutrition Information:
Calories Per Serving: 398 calories, Total Fat: 23g, Cholesterol: 102 mg, Sodium: 373 mg, Total Carbohydrates: 32g, Fiber: 4g, Sugars: 1g, Protein 14g.

8. Fettuccine Carbonara

Fettuccine Carbonara is an Italian dish made with pasta, egg, cheese, and bacon. It is the perfect combination of flavors and textures for a delicious meal.

Serving: 4
Preparation Time: 10 minutes
Ready Time: 20 minutes

Ingredients:
- 8 oz uncooked fettuccine noodles
- 2 tablespoons olive oil
- 4 slices bacon, diced
- 2 cloves garlic, minced
- 1/4 cup white wine
- 2 eggs
- 1/2 cup grated Parmesan cheese
- 2 tablespoons chopped fresh parsley
- Salt and pepper, to taste

Instructions:
1. Bring a large pot of salted water to a boil and add the fettuccine noodles. Cook until al dente, about 10 minutes. Drain and set aside.
2. In a large skillet over medium heat, heat the olive oil. Once heated, add the diced bacon and cook until golden and crispy, about 7-8 minutes. Add the garlic and cook for 1 minute longer.
3. Pour in the white wine and cook until the liquid has reduced by half.
4. In a medium bowl, combine the eggs and Parmesan cheese.
5. Once the wine has finished reducing, pour the eggs and cheese over the bacon and garlic in the skillet.
6. Add the cooked noodles to the mixture and toss quickly to coat with sauce.
7. Stir in the parsley and season with salt and pepper to taste.

Nutrition Information: Calories: 370, Total Fat: 17 g, Saturated Fat: 6.7 g, Cholesterol: 95 mg, Sodium: 712 mg, Carbohydrates: 33 g, Fiber: 1.7 g, Sugars: 0.5 g, Protein: 17 g.

9. Penne Carbonara

Penne Carbonara is a classic Italian dish that combines al dente penne pasta with rich creamy carbonara sauce. The silky sauce, made of egg yolks, parmesan cheese, and salty pancetta, envelopes the pasta for a wonderful meal.

Serving: 4

Preparation Time: 10 minutes

Ready Time: 20 minutes

Ingredients:
- 2 tablespoons olive oil
- 4 ounces crumbled pancetta
- 1/2 teaspoon black pepper
- 1/4 cup chopped onion
- 3 cloves minced garlic
- 2 eggs
- 1/2 cup grated Parmesan cheese
- 2 1/2 tablespoons butter
- 8 ounces of penne pasta
- 2 tablespoons chopped fresh parsley

Instructions:
1. Heat a large skillet over medium-high heat. Add the olive oil, pancetta, pepper, onion, and garlic. Saute for 5 minutes, or until the onions and pancetta are lightly browned.
2. In a bowl, whisk together the eggs and Parmesan cheese.
3. Reduce the heat to low and add the butter and the egg mixture. Stir until the butter is melted and the eggs are slightly cooked.
4. Cook the penne according to package directions. Drain the pasta, reserving 1/4 cup of the cooking liquid.
5. Add the penne to the skillet and toss to combine with the sauce. If the sauce is too thick, add some of the reserved cooking liquid. Sprinkle with the parsley and serve.

Nutrition Information: Calories: 479; Total Fat: 31.6g; Cholesterol: 87.2mg; Sodium: 619.9mg; Total Carbohydrate: 32.5g; Protein: 14.3g

10. Farfalle Carbonara

Farfalle Carbonara is an Italian classic dish. This dish combines chunks of bacon, Parmesan cheese, eggs, and parsley with farfalle (bowtie) pasta to create a creamy and satisfying meal.
Serving: 6
Preparation Time: 10 minutes
Ready Time: 40 minutes

Ingredients:
- 8 ounces uncooked farfalle pasta
- 6 slices bacon, chopped
- 1 cup freshly grated Parmesan cheese
- 3 eggs
- 1/4 cup chopped parsley
- Salt and pepper to taste

Instructions:
1. Cook the farfalle pasta according to the package Instructions. Drain and set aside.
2. In a large skillet over medium-high heat, cook the bacon until crispy.
3. In a medium bowl, whisk together the Parmesan cheese, eggs, parsley and salt and pepper.
4. Add the cooked pasta and bacon to the egg mixture and mix until evenly combined.
5. Return the pasta mixture to the skillet and cook until the eggs are set, about 5 minutes, stirring occasionally.

Nutrition Information:
Per Serving: Calories: 418 kcal, Carbohydrates: 40 g, Protein: 16 g, Fat: 21 g, Saturated Fat: 9 g, Cholesterol: 116 mg, Sodium: 472 mg, Potassium: 191 mg, Fiber: 1 g, Sugar: 1 g, Vitamin A: 545 IU, Vitamin C: 1 mg, Calcium: 138 mg, Iron: 1 mg.

11. Gnocchi Carbonara

Gnocchi Carbonara is an Italian dish made with gnocchi, bacon, eggs, Parmesan cheese, and black pepper. This creamy, savory dish is a quick and easy weeknight meal that comes together in just about 25 minutes!
Serving: 4

Preparation time: 10 minutes
Ready time: 15 minutes

Ingredients:
- 1 lb. package of gnocchi
- 1/4 cup of bacon, diced
- 2 eggs, whisked
- 1/4 cup of Parmesan cheese
- 1/8 teaspoon of black pepper
- Salt to taste

Instructions:
1. Heat a pot of salted boiling water until it boils. Then add in the package of gnocchi and cook until they float to the top. Drain the gnocchi in a colander and set aside.

2. In a large skillet or pan, cook the bacon over medium heat until crisp. Using a slotted spoon, transfer the bacon onto a paper towel. Reserve the bacon fat in the skillet.
3. Add the cooked gnocchi to the skillet with the bacon fat and cook for about 2 minutes or until lightly browned.
4. In a medium bowl, whisk together the eggs and Parmesan cheese until they are combined.
5. Reduce the heat to low and pour the egg and cheese mixture over the gnocchi and bacon. Stir everything together until the eggs are cooked and the mixture is creamy.
6. Add black pepper to taste, and salt if desired. Serve hot.

Nutrition Information: per serving (about 1/4 of the dish):
Calories: 266, Fat: 10 grams, Protein: 11.4 grams, Carbohydrates: 32.1 grams, Fiber: 2.6 grams

12. Ziti Carbonara

Ziti Carbonara is an Italian pasta dish that is creamy and savory, made with ziti pasta and tossed in a bacon and parmesan cheese sauce.
Serving: 8
Preparation Time: 15 minutes

Ready Time: 45 minutes

Ingredients:
- 2 tablespoons olive oil
- 1/2 pound bacon, chopped
- 1/2 cup minced onion
- 2 cloves of garlic, minced
- 8 ounces ziti pasta
- 2 eggs
- 2 cup half-and-half
- 1/2 cup grated Parmesan cheese
- Salt and black pepper to taste
- Chopped fresh parsley for garnish

Instructions:
1. Preheat oven to 350 degrees F.
2. Heat olive oil in a large skillet over medium heat. Add bacon, onion, and garlic and cook, stirring occasionally, until bacon is crisp and golden, about 8 minutes.
3. Meanwhile, bring a large pot of salted water to a boil. Cook ziti until al dente, about 8 minutes.
4. In a medium bowl, whisk together eggs and half-and-half.
5. When bacon is done, drain off all fat from skillet. Reduce heat to low.
6. Drain ziti and add to skillet. Pour egg mixture over ziti and stir to combine.
7. Add Parmesan cheese and season with salt and pepper. Stir until cheese is melted.
8. Transfer carbonara to a 9-inch baking dish.
9. Bake for 25 minutes. Let cool for 10 minutes before garnishing with parsley and serving.

Nutrition Information: Per serving, Ziti Carbonara has 350 calories, 19 grams of fat, 8 grams of saturated fat, 155 milligrams of cholesterol, 353 milligrams of sodium, 25 grams of carbohydrates, and 15 grams of protein.

13. Fusilli Carbonara

Fusilli Carbonara is a classic Italian pasta dish featuring pancetta, eggs, cream, and cheese. Serve it with a simple tossed salad for an easy weeknight supper.
Serving: 4
Preparation time: 10 minutes
Ready time: 20 minutes

Ingredients:
- 8 ounces fusilli pasta
- 4 slices pancetta, diced
- 1/4 cup freshly grated Parmigiano-Reggiano cheese plus more for serving
- 2 eggs
- 1/4 cup heavy cream
- 2 tablespoons butter
- Salt and pepper, to taste

Instructions:
1. Bring a pot of salted water to a boil. Add the fusilli and cook according to package Instructions.
2. Meanwhile, in a large skillet over medium heat, add the pancetta and cook until lightly browned and crispy, about 5 minutes.
3. In a bowl, whisk together the Parmigiano-Reggiano cheese, eggs, and cream.
4. Drain the pasta and add it to the skillet with the pancetta. Turn the heat to low and add the butter.
5. Pour the egg mixture over the pasta and stir to coat. Allow the eggs to cook until they are glossy and thick, about 5 minutes.
6. Serve the pasta with extra Parmigiano-Reggiano cheese, salt, and pepper.

Nutrition Information:
Calories: 414; Fat: 15g; Carbs: 60g; Protein: 13g

14. Macaroni Carbonara

Macaroni Carbonara is a classic Italian pasta dish. With just a few simple Ingredients, it's a rich and creamy dish that is surprisingly easy to make in just a few minutes.

Serving: 4 servings
Preparation Time: 10 minutes
Ready Time: 20 minutes

Ingredients:
- 8 ounces macaroni
- ¼ cup Parmesan cheese, grated
- 2 tablespoons butter
- 2 tablespoons olive oil
- 2 cloves garlic, minced
- 1 teaspoon salt
- ½ teaspoon ground black pepper
- ½ cup heavy cream
- 1 egg yolk
- 2 tablespoons parsley, chopped

Instructions:
1. Bring a large pot of salted water to a boil and cook the macaroni until al dente according to the package Instructions.
2. Meanwhile, in a medium saucepan, heat the butter and olive oil over medium heat. Add the garlic, salt, and pepper, and cook for 1 minute.
3. Add the heavy cream and bring to a simmer.
4. In a small bowl, whisk together the egg yolk and Parmesan cheese.
5. Once the macaroni is done, add it to the saucepan with the cream mixture and reduce the heat to low.
6. Quickly whisk in the egg-Parmesan mixture until combined.
7. Mix in the parsley and season to taste.
8. Serve immediately.

Nutrition Information: Per Serving: Calories 284; Total Fat 11g; Cholesterol 59mg; Sodium 519mg; Potassium 40mg; Total Carbohydrates 30g; Dietary Fiber 1g; Sugars 2g; Protein 10g.

15. Tagliatelle Carbonara

Creamy and indulgent, Tagliatelle Carbonara is a classic Italian dish. The combination of salty bacon, rich cream, and savory Parmesan cheese creates a flavor and texture combo that will have your taste buds dancing!

Serving: Serves 4
Preparation Time: 10 minutes
Ready Time: 20 minutes

Ingredients:
- 8 ounces tagliatelle pasta
- 2 slices bacon, diced
- 2 cloves garlic, minced
- 2 tablespoons olive oil
- 2 eggs
- 1/4 cup heavy cream
- 1/4 cup grated Parmesan cheese
- Salt and pepper, to taste

Instructions:
1. Bring a pot of salted water to a boil, then cook the tagliatelle pasta according to the package directions.
2. Heat a large skillet over medium-low heat. Add the bacon and cook until crisp and golden brown.
3. Add the garlic and olive oil to the skillet and cook until fragrant, about 2 minutes.
4. In a separate bowl, whisk together the eggs and cream.
5. Drain the cooked pasta and add it to the skillet with the bacon and garlic. Increase the heat to medium and cook, stirring frequently, until the pasta is warmed through, about 2-3 minutes.
6. Add the egg and cream mixture to the skillet and stir to combine. Remove the skillet from the heat and stir in the Parmesan cheese.
7. Season with salt and pepper to taste and serve.

Nutrition Information:
Calories: 331 kcal, Carbohydrates: 28 g, Protein: 12 g, Fat: 17 g, Saturated Fat: 6 g, Cholesterol: 85 mg, Sodium: 285 mg, Potassium: 97 mg, Fiber: 1 g, Sugar: 1 g, Vitamin A: 282 IU, Vitamin C: 1 mg, Calcium: 57 mg, Iron: 1 mg

16. Lasagna Carbonara

Lasagna Carbonara
A rich and creamy Italian dish, Lasagna Carbonara is a classic pasta dish sure to delight your family. It features lasagna noodles layered with a creamy Parmesan and ricotta cheese sauce, bacon, and zucchini. This delicious dish comes together in an hour and feeds four and provides an excellent source of protein.
Serving: 4
Preparation Time: 15 minutes
Ready Time: 45 minutes

Ingredients:
- 9 lasagna sheets
- 2 tablespoons olive oil
- 1 onion, diced
- 3 cloves garlic, minced
- 2 cups cooked bacon, finely diced
- 4 cups ricotta cheese
- 1/2 cup white wine
- 1/4 cup grated Parmesan cheese
- 1/3 cup chopped parsley
- 1 zucchini, thinly sliced
- 1/2 teaspoon ground black pepper
- 1/2 teaspoon salt

Instructions:
1. Preheat oven to 350 degrees F. Grease a 9-inch baking dish and set aside.
2. Bring a large pot of salted water to a boil. Add the lasagna sheets and cook until al dente, about 7 to 8 minutes. Drain the noodles and rinse with cold water to stop the cooking process.
3. Heat the olive oil in a medium-sized skillet set over medium-high heat. Add the onions and garlic and sauté until softened, about 5 minutes. Add the bacon and cook for another 3 minutes.
4. In a large bowl, stir together the ricotta cheese, white wine, Parmesan cheese, parsley, zucchini, black pepper, and salt.
5. Arrange the cooked lasagna noodles in the greased dish. Spread half of the ricotta cheese mixture over the noodles. Top with half of the bacon mixture.

Repeat with the remaining noodles, ricotta cheese mixture, and bacon mixture.
6. Bake in the preheated oven for 35 to 45 minutes, or until golden and bubbly. Let stand 10 minutes before serving.

Nutrition Information: Each serving contains approximately 225 calories, 15 grams fat, 16 grams protein, and 9 grams carbohydrates.

17. Cannelloni Carbonara

Try this restaurant-style Cannelloni Carbonara recipe for a delicious weeknight dinner, the perfect balance between indulgent and light.
Serving: 8
Preparation time: 25 minutes
Ready time: 1 hour

Ingredients:
- 12 cannelloni tubes
- 800g minced beef
- 500ml double cream
- 2 onions, diced
- 2 cloves of garlic, minced
- 300g diced bacon
- 300g grated Parmesan cheese
- 1/2 tsp of chilli flakes
- Salt and pepper to taste

Instructions:
1. Preheat your oven to 190°C and lightly grease a baking dish.
2. Boil the cannelloni tubes in salted water for about 5 minutes or until al dente.
3. Mix the minced beef with the diced onion, garlic, bacon, and chilli and season with salt and pepper.
4. Spread a layer of the mixture over the bottom of the greased baking dish and top it with a layer of cannelloni tubes.
5. Spread the remaining mixture over the cannelloni and top it with the double cream.

6. Sprinkle the Parmesan cheese over the top before baking in the preheated oven for 40 minutes or until golden brown.

Nutrition Information:
Per serving: 323 Calories, 19.3g Fat, 16.6g Protein, 4.7g Carbs, 1.5g Fibre.

18. Stuffed Shells Carbonara

Stuffed Shells Carbonara is an Italian classic that is sure to delight. A hearty comfort food made with pancetta, cheese, and creamy sauce, this dish is comforting, delicious, and easy to make.
Serving: 8
Preparation Time: 20 minutes
Ready Time: 45 minutes

Ingredients:
- 1 pound jumbo pasta shells
- 2 tablespoons olive oil
- 4 ounces diced pancetta
- 2 cloves garlic, minced
- 1/2 cup finely grated Parmesan cheese
- 2 cups ricotta cheese
- 1 large egg
- 2 tablespoons Italian parsley, roughly chopped
- 1 teaspoon salt
- 1/2 teaspoon black pepper
- 4 and 1/2 cups homemade or store-bought marinara sauce
- 1/2 cup shredded mozzarella cheese

Instructions:
1. Preheat oven to 375 degrees F.
2. Bring a large pot of salted water to a boil. Cook shells for about 8 minutes, until al dente. Drain and set aside.
3. Heat olive oil in a large skillet over medium heat. Add pancetta and garlic and sauté until golden brown, about 5 minutes.
4. Remove from heat and add Parmesan, ricotta, egg, parsley, salt and pepper. Stir until combined.

5. Spread 3 cups of marinara sauce on the bottom of a 9x13-inch baking dish.

6. Stuff each cooked shell with a heaping tablespoon of the pancetta mixture. Place shells in the baking dish, top with remaining marinara sauce and mozzarella cheese.

7. Bake in preheated oven for 25 minutes, until cheese is melted and bubbly.

Nutrition Information:
Calories: 261, Fat: 10g, Cholesterol: 38mg, Sodium: 900mg, Carbohydrates: 28g, Protein: 13g

19. Carbonara Pizza

Carbonara Pizza is a delicious variation of traditional Italian pizza. It features creamy carbonara sauce, mozzarella cheese, and bacon strips for a perfectly savory and indulgent meal.
Serving: 4
Preparation Time: 20 minutes
Ready Time: 20-25 minutes

Ingredients:
- Pizza Dough
- Carbonara Sauce
- Mozzarella Cheese
- Bacon Strips
- Fresh Parsley (optional)

Instructions:
1) Preheat the oven to 425°F.
2) Roll out the pizza dough on a baking sheet lined with parchment paper.
3) Spread the carbonara sauce evenly over the top.
4) Sprinkle mozzarella cheese and bacon strips over the pizza.
5) Bake for 20-25 minutes, or until the crust is golden and the cheese is bubbly.
6) Garnish with fresh parsley (optional).

Nutrition Information (per serving):
Calories: 350
Carbohydrates: 41g
Protein: 16g
Fat: 14g

20. Carbonara Calzone

Carbonara Calzone is a twist on traditional Italian pizza, and it's sure to be a hit! This delicious recipe is a delicious mix of classic Italian flavours, with bacon, garlic, cream and Parmesan cheese all baked inside a calzone-style pizza. A great dish to share with friends and family, this recipe serves 8 people and should take approximately 20 minutes of preparation, before it is ready to bake and enjoy in 25 minutes.
Serving: 8
Preparation Time: 20 minutes
Ready Time: 25 minutes

Ingredients:
- 2 cups all-purpose flour
- 2 teaspoons active dry yeast
- 1 teaspoon salt
- 1 cup lukewarm water
- 7 ounces cooked bacon, diced
- 2 cloves garlic, minced
- 2 eggs
- ½ cup heavy cream
- ½ cup grated Parmesan cheese
- 2 tablespoons olive oil

Instructions:
1. In a large bowl, mix together the flour, yeast, and salt.
2. Pour in the lukewarm water and mix until a rough dough forms.
3. Turn the dough onto a lightly floured surface, and knead it for 5 minutes.
4. In a medium bowl, combine the bacon, garlic, eggs, cream, and Parmesan cheese.
5. Preheat oven to 375 degrees Fahrenheit.

6. Turn the pizza dough onto a lightly floured surface and roll it out into a 16-inch round.
7. Place the pizza dough onto a lightly floured baking sheet.
8. Spread the bacon mixture in the middle of the dough, leaving a 2-inch border.
9. Fold the border up over the filling, forming a calzone shape.
10. Brush the top of the crust with olive oil.
11. Bake for 25 minutes, or until golden brown.
12. Slice and serve immediately.

Nutrition Information: Calories: 274, Fat: 11.8g, Cholesterol: 78mg, Sodium: 643mg, Carbohydrates: 24.3g, Fiber: 1.2g, Sugar: 0.9g, Protein: 13.4g

21. Carbonara Stromboli

Carbonara Stromboli
Serving: 8
Preparation Time: 20 minutes
Ready Time: 40 minutes

Ingredients:
• 2 tablespoons olive oil
• 5 cloves garlic, minced
• 1 teaspoon Italian seasoning
• 2 cups mozzarella cheese, divided
• 1 cup Parmesan cheese, divided
• 1/4 teaspoon black pepper
• 1/4 teaspoon sea salt
• 2 tablespoons chopped fresh parsley
• 1/2 cup red bell pepper, diced
• 1/2 cup cooked bacon, diced
• Pizza dough
• 2 eggs, lightly beaten

Instructions:
1. Preheat the oven to 425°F.
2. In a small skillet, heat the olive oil.

3. Sauté the garlic and Italian seasoning for about 1 minute, until aromatic.
4. In a small bowl, combine 1 cup of the mozzarella cheese, 1/2 cup of the Parmesan cheese, pepper, salt, parsley, bell pepper, and bacon. Stir until well blended.
5. Roll out the pizza dough into a 12 inch circle.
6. Transfer the dough to a pizza pan.
7. Top the dough with the cheese and bacon mixture.
8. Drizzle the garlic and oil mixture over the top.
9. Top the pizza with the remaining 1 cup of mozzarella cheese and 1/2 cup of Parmesan cheese.
10. Fold the edges of the pizza dough over the toppings to create a stromboli.
11. Brush the top of the stromboli with the beaten eggs.
12. Bake for 20-25 minutes, or until golden.

Nutrition Information:
Calories: 310, Total Fat: 16g, Saturated Fat: 7g, Trans Fat: 0g,,
Cholesterol: 85mg, Sodium: 855mg, Carbohydrates: 23g, Fiber: 2g, Sugar: 2g, Protein: 15g

22. Carbonara Bruschetta

Carbonara Bruschetta is an Italian-style bruschetta dish that combines succulent and creamy carbonara sauce with fragrant bruschetta. Enjoy this delicious recipe to transform ordinary bruschetta into a sophisticated delight.
Serving: 4
Preparation Time: 15 minutes
Ready Time: 15 minutes

Ingredients:
- 2 English muffins, halved and lightly toasted
- 1/2 cup cooked spaghetti
- 2 tablespoons bacon bits
- 1/2 cup carbonara sauce
- 1/4 cup grated cheese

Instructions:
1. Preheat oven to 350°F (175°C).
2. Place each muffin half cut-side up on a foil-lined baking tray.
3. Top each muffin with cooked spaghetti, bacon bits, carbonara sauce, and grated cheese.
4. Bake for 15 minutes until the cheese is melted and bubbling.
5. Serve the Carbonara Bruschetta hot.

Nutrition Information:
Calories: 311, Fat: 8.7g, Saturated Fat: 2.5g, Cholesterol: 15mg, Sodium: 517mg, Carbohydrates: 42.7g, Fiber: 2.4g, Sugar: 1.5g, Protein: 12.3g

23. Carbonara Garlic Bread

Carbonara Garlic Bread is a unique dish that combines the delicious flavors of garlic and carbonara sauce with the crunch of toasted bread. It's a perfect side dish or meal in itself!
Serving Size: 4
Preparation Time: 20 minutes
Ready Time: 25 minutes

Ingredients:
- 4 cloves garlic, minced
- 4 slices of white bread, toasted
- 2 tablespoons butter
- ⅓ cup carbonara sauce
- 2 tablespoons fresh parsley, minced
- ¼ teaspoon black pepper
- ¼ teaspoon paprika

Instructions:
1. Preheat oven to 350°F.
2. In a large skillet, sauté minced garlic in butter over medium heat until garlic is softened and aromatic.
3. Place toasted bread slices on a baking sheet. Spread carbonara sauce over each slice.
4. Top each slice with garlic and butter mixture. Sprinkle each slice with parsley, black pepper, and paprika.

5. Bake for 15 minutes until garlic and bread are lightly browned.

Nutrition Information: Per serving (1 slice):
- Calories: 189
- Total Fat: 11.3g
- Carbohydrates: 17.7g
- Protein: 6.6g

24. Carbonara Flatbread

Carbonara Flatbread
Serving: 4
Preparation Time: 10 minutes
Ready Time: 15 minutes

Ingredients:
- 1 pre-made flatbread
- 4 tablespoons Alfredo sauce
- 2 cups cooked and crumbled bacon
- 2 cups shredded mozzarella cheese
- Fresh parsley leaves, chopped (optional)

Instructions:
1. Preheat oven to 350 degrees Fahrenheit.
2. Place flatbread on an oven-safe baking sheet.
3. Spread each piece of flatbread with Alfredo sauce.
4. Top with cooked and crumbled bacon.
5. Sprinkle with mozzarella cheese.
6. Bake in preheated oven for 8-10 minutes, until cheese is melted and flatbread is heated through.
7. Garnish with fresh chopped parsley, if desired.

Nutrition Information:
Serving size: 1 piece
Calories: 305
Total fat: 15.3 g
Saturated fat: 7.3 g
Cholesterol: 53 mg

Sodium: 722 mg
Carbohydrates: 24.8 g
Fiber: 1.2 g
Protein: 15.2 g

25. Carbonara Panini

Carbonara Panini is an Italian-style pressed sandwich with creamy Carbonara-style fillings, oozing out from between two toasty slices of bread. This savory and satisfying dish is a great way to spice up your lunch and can be enjoyed as a main or as a side.
Serving: 2
Preparation Time: 15 minutes
Ready Time: 25 minutes

Ingredients:
- 4 slices sourdough bread
- 4 tablespoons olive oil
- 3 garlic cloves, minced
- ½ cup diced pancetta
- 1 cup cooked spaghetti
- 1/4 cup grated Parmesan cheese
- 2 whole eggs
- 1/4 teaspoon black pepper
- 2 tablespoons freshly chopped parsley

Instructions:
1. Heat 1 tablespoon of olive oil over medium-high heat in a skillet. Add the garlic and stir for about a minute until fragrant.
2. Add the pancetta and sauté until it browns slightly and the fat begins to render out, about 5 minutes.
3. Add the cooked spaghetti to the pan, stir to combine, and cook for a few minutes until heated through.
4. Remove the pan from the heat and add the Parmesan cheese, eggs, pepper, parsley, and 1 tablespoon of olive oil. Stir to combine until the cheese has melted and the eggs become creamy.
5. Heat a separate skillet over medium-high heat and add the remaining 2 tablespoons of olive oil.

6. Toast each slice of bread in the skillet until golden brown and crispy, about 2 minutes per side.
7. Place the toasted bread on a cutting board and spread the Carbonara mixture evenly over each slice of bread.
8. Place the filled bread slices in the skillet and cook for 2 minutes per side, flipping carefully.
9. Serve the Carbonara Paninis hot and enjoy!

Nutrition Information (per serving):
Calories: 495
Fat: 30.2 g
Carbohydrates: 27.9 g
Protein: 23.3 g

26. Carbonara Sandwich

Carbonara Sandwich
Serving: 2
Preparation Time: 10 minutes
Ready Time: 10 minutes

Ingredients:
- 2 slices of the bread of your choice
- 2 slices of bacon, chopped
- 2 eggs, whisked in a bowl
- 2 tablespoons of grated Parmesan cheese
- Salt & pepper for taste
- 2 tablespoons of olive oil

Instructions:
1. Heat up the oil in a pan over medium heat and add the bacon, cook until crispy.
2. Meanwhile, toast the bread slices and set aside.
3. Once the bacon is cooked, remove it from the pan and lower the heat to low.
4. Whisk 1 tablespoon of Parmesan cheese into the eggs and season with salt and pepper.

5. Pour the eggs into the pan with the bacon grease and let it cook slowly.

6. Once everything is cooked through, assemble the sandwich by placing one slice of bread and adding the bacon and egg mixture.

7. Add the Parmesan cheese over the sandwich and top it with the second slice of bread.

8. Serve immediately.

Nutrition Information:
Calories: 300 kcal,
Total Fat: 20 g,
Saturated Fat: 5 g,
Carbohydrates: 16 g,
Protein: 13 g

27. Carbonara Crostini

This Carbonara Crostini recipe is a creamy and savory twist on toast and makes an elegant appetizer or light dinner.
SERVING
Servings: 6
PREPARATION TIME
Prep Time: 10 minutes
READY TIME
Ready Time: 30 minutes

Ingredients:
• 2 slices thick-cut bacon, chopped
• 2 cloves garlic, minced
• 2 tablespoons onion, diced
• 1/2 teaspoon salt
• 1/4 teaspoon black pepper
• 2 tablespoons butter
• 1/4 cup half-and-half cream
• 1 large egg
• 1/4 cup Parmesan cheese, grated
• 6 slices Italian bread
• 2 tablespoons parsley, chopped (for garnish)

Instructions:
1. Preheat oven to 350F.
2. In a medium skillet over medium-high heat, cook bacon until crisp, about 5-7 minutes.
3. Add garlic, onion, salt, and pepper to the pan and cook until fragrant, about 1 minute.
4. Turn off the heat and stir in butter, half-and-half cream, egg, and Parmesan cheese until combined.
5. Place bread slices on a baking sheet and spoon the carbonara mixture onto the top of each one.
6. Bake for 15-20 minutes, or until the edges of the crostini are golden and cheese is melted.
7. Garnish with chopped parsley, if desired, and serve warm.

Nutrition Information
Calories: 274 kcal | Carbohydrates: 19g | Protein: 8g | Fat: 19g | Saturated Fat: 9g | Cholesterol: 59mg | Sodium: 336mg | Potassium: 69mg | Fiber: 1g | Sugar: 2g | Vitamin A: 456IU | Vitamin C: 1mg | Calcium: 97mg | Iron: 1mg

28. Carbonara Dip

This carbonara dip is a creamy, cheesy classic with just the right amount of flavor. It's simple to make and perfect as an appetizer for both parties or snacks!
Serving: 4
Preparation time: 10 minutes
Ready time: 10 minutes

Ingredients:
- 2 tablespoons of butter
- 6 slices of bacon
- 2 tablespoons of all-purpose flour
- 1 ½ cups of milk
- 2 cups of grated Parmesan cheese
- 3 cloves of garlic, chopped
- 2 teaspoons of Italian seasoning

- ¼ teaspoon of ground black pepper

Instructions:
1. Preheat oven to 425F. Heat a skillet over medium heat.
2. Add the bacon and cook until crispy, about 5 minutes. Remove the bacon from the pan and set aside.
3. Add the butter to the skillet and melt. Add the flour and stir for 1 minute.
4. Gradually add the milk, whisking constantly until the mixture thickens. Add the Parmesan cheese and stir until melted.
5. Stir in garlic, Italian seasoning, and black pepper.
6. Pour the dip into a baking dish and bake in the preheated oven for 10 minutes.
7. Remove from oven and top with bacon. Serve and enjoy.

Nutrition Information: Calories per serving: 494; Total fat: 33 g; Sodium: 1164 mg; Total carbohydrates: 14 g; Protein: 32 g;

29. Carbonara Salad

Carbonara Salad is a delicious and creamy pasta salad. This dish is full of flavor and a great crowd pleaser. It's easy to make and perfect for a weeknight dinner or summer party.
Serving: 6
Preparation Time: 25 minutes
Ready Time: 25 minutes

Ingredients:
- 2 (16-ounce) boxes penne pasta
- 1/2 cup bacon pieces
- 1/2 cup Parmesan cheese, grated
- 2 cloves garlic, chopped
- 2 cups heavy cream
- 4 eggs, beaten
- Salt and pepper, to taste
- 2 tablespoons chopped fresh Italian parsley

Instructions:

1. Cook the penne pasta according to the Instructions on the package.
2. In a large skillet over medium heat, cook the bacon until it is crispy. Drain off the fat.
3. Reduce the heat to low and add the Parmesan cheese, garlic, and heavy cream. Stir until the cheese is melted and the mixture is creamy.
4. Raise the heat to medium and add the beaten eggs. Stir constantly until the eggs are cooked.
5. Remove from the heat and season with salt and pepper.
6. In a large bowl, combine the cooked penne pasta, creamy egg mixture, and bacon pieces. Mix well.
7. Sprinkle with chopped parsley.
8. Serve while hot.

Nutrition Information:
Calories: 458 kcal, Carbohydrates: 46 g, Protein: 16 g, Fat: 23 g, Saturated Fat: 12 g, Cholesterol: 133 mg, Sodium: 398 mg, Potassium: 208 mg, Fiber: 3 g, Sugar: 2 g, Vitamin A: 641 IU, Vitamin C: 2 mg, Calcium: 190 mg, Iron: 1 mg

30. Carbonara Deviled Eggs

Carbonara Deviled Eggs are a surprisingly easy and tasty dish with an Italian twist! This twist on the classic deviled egg pairs creamy egg yolks with the salty flavors of classic carbonara.
Serving: 12 deviled eggs
Preparation Time: 15 minutes
Ready Time: 15 minutes

Ingredients:
- 6 hard boiled eggs, peeled
- 2 tablespoons of cream cheese
- 2 tablespoons of mayonnaise
- 2 tablespoons of freshly grated Parmesan
- 2 teaspoons of Dijon mustard
- 2 teaspoons of minced garlic
- 2 slices of cooked bacon, diced
- Salt and pepper to taste

Instructions:
1. Slice the hard boiled eggs in half and scoop the egg yolks into a bowl.
2. Mash the egg yolks with a fork.
3. Add the cream cheese, mayonnaise, Parmesan, Dijon mustard, garlic, bacon, salt and pepper and mix until the Ingredients are combined.
4. Spoon the mixture into the egg whites and top with extra bacon.
5. Refrigerate the eggs for at least 15 minutes before serving.

Nutrition Information:
Calories: 84, Fat: 6.3g, Carbs: 0.9g, Protein: 5.4g

31. Carbonara Stuffed Mushrooms

Indulge in the irresistible flavors of Carbonara Stuffed Mushrooms. This unique twist on the classic Italian pasta dish combines the creamy and rich carbonara sauce with earthy mushrooms for a mouthwatering appetizer or side dish. Each mushroom cap is filled with a decadent mixture of bacon, cheese, eggs, and herbs, creating a savory delight that is sure to impress. Whether you're hosting a dinner party or looking for a delicious appetizer, these Carbonara Stuffed Mushrooms are guaranteed to be a crowd-pleaser.
Serving: 4 servings
Preparation Time: 20 minutes
Ready Time: 35 minutes

Ingredients:
- 8 large mushrooms (such as cremini or button mushrooms)
- 4 slices bacon, cooked and crumbled
- 1/2 cup grated Parmesan cheese
- 2 eggs
- 2 tablespoons chopped fresh parsley
- 2 cloves garlic, minced
- 1/4 teaspoon salt
- 1/4 teaspoon black pepper
- Fresh parsley, chopped (for garnish)

Instructions:

1. Preheat the oven to 375°F (190°C). Line a baking sheet with parchment paper.
2. Remove the stems from the mushrooms and gently scoop out the gills to create space for the stuffing. Set the mushroom caps aside.
3. In a mixing bowl, combine the crumbled bacon, grated Parmesan cheese, eggs, chopped fresh parsley, minced garlic, salt, and black pepper. Mix well until all the ingredients are evenly incorporated.
4. Fill each mushroom cap generously with the carbonara mixture, pressing it down slightly to ensure it fills the cavity.
5. Place the stuffed mushrooms on the prepared baking sheet and bake in the preheated oven for 15-18 minutes, or until the mushrooms are tender and the filling is golden and slightly puffed.
6. Remove from the oven and let the mushrooms cool for a few minutes.
7. Garnish with fresh chopped parsley and serve the Carbonara Stuffed Mushrooms warm.

Nutrition Information (per serving):
Calories: 173
Fat: 11g
Saturated Fat: 5g
Cholesterol: 121mg
Sodium: 502mg
Carbohydrates: 5g
Fiber: 1g
Sugar: 1g
Protein: 14g
Note: The nutrition information is approximate and may vary depending on the specific ingredients used.

32. Carbonara Stuffed Peppers

Carbonara Stuffed Peppers is a flavorful twist on the traditional Italian recipe, stuffed with carbonara sauce and cheese. Perfect for a hearty weeknight meal!
Serving: 4
Preparation Time: 15 minutes
Ready Time: 25 minutes

Ingredients:
- 4 large bell peppers
- 2 cups cooked penne pasta
- 3/4 cup carbonara sauce
- 1/2 cup shredded mozzarella cheese
- 2 tablespoons freshly chopped parsley

Instructions:
1. Preheat oven to 375F.
2. Slice off the tops of the bell peppers and remove the seeds and membranes.
3. Place the peppers in a large baking dish.
4. In a large bowl, mix together the cooked penne pasta, carbonara sauce, mozzarella cheese and parsley.
5. Divide the mixture into the 4 bell peppers, overfilling the peppers slightly.
6. Bake for 20-25 minutes, or until the peppers are tender and the cheese is melted.
7. Serve hot.

Nutrition Information: Per Serving: 229 calories; 10.1 g fat; 25.4 g carbohydrates; 5.4 g protein; 7.5 g fiber.

33. Carbonara Stuffed Tomatoes

Carbonara Stuffed Tomatoes are a delicious twist to traditional Italian Carbonara. They are the perfect combination of classic Carbonara flavors in a stuffed tomato.
Serving: 4
Preparation time: 20 minutes
Ready time: 40 minutes

Ingredients:
- 4 large tomatoes
- 8 bacon strips
- 1/4 cup minced onion
- 1/2 cup peas
- 4 cloves garlic, minced

- 4 eggs
- 1/3 cup Parmesan cheese
- 2 tablespoons olive oil
- Salt and pepper to taste

Instructions:
1. Preheat oven to 375°F.
2. Cut the top of each tomato and scoop out the insides. Discard the seeds and reserve the tomatoes.
3. In a large skillet, heat olive oil over medium heat. Add bacon strips and cook until crisp.
4. Add the garlic and onion to the pan and cook until softened.
5. Add the peas to the pan and cook for 2 minutes.
6. In a small bowl, whisk together the eggs and Parmesan cheese.
7. Fill each tomato with the cooked bacon mixture and pour the egg and Parmesan mixture over top.
8. Place the tomatoes in a baking dish and bake for 25 minutes.
9. Let cool for 5 minutes before serving.

Nutrition Information:
Calories: 501
Fat: 33g
Carbohydrates: 18g
Protein: 32g
Sodium: 523mg
Fiber: 4g

34. Carbonara Stuffed Zucchini

Carbonara Stuffed Zucchini is an easy, delicious and healthy dish to make. It is stuffed with bacon, cheese, mushrooms, and onions and is sure to be a hit at your next gathering.
Serving: 4
Preparation Time: 15 minutes
Ready Time: 30 minutes

Ingredients:
- Olive oil

- 4 medium zucchinis
- 2 cloves of garlic, minced
- 8 strips bacon, diced
- ½ cup mushrooms, chopped
- ½ cup yellow onion, diced
- 2 cups mozzarella cheese, grated
- ½ cup parmesan cheese, grated
- ½ teaspoon Italian seasoning
- Salt and pepper, to taste

Instructions:
1. Preheat oven to 375 degrees Fahrenheit.
2. Cut each zucchini in half and scoop out the middle with a spoon.
3. Heat oil in a large skillet over medium-high. Add garlic and stir for 2 minutes.
4. Add bacon, mushrooms, and onions and sauté until the bacon is crispy.
5. Remove mixture from heat and stir in mozzarella and parmesan cheese and Italian seasoning.
6. Season with salt and pepper.
7. Stuff each zucchini half with the cheese mixture and place in a baking dish.
8. Bake for 20-30 minutes until the zucchini is cooked through.

Nutrition Information:
Calories: 246, Fat: 14g, Carbohydrates: 14.3g, Protein: 17g, Fiber: 3.3g

35. Carbonara Stuffed Squash

Carbonara Stuffed Squash is a twist on traditional carbonara featuring roasted squash stuffed with a creamy and flavorful egg and cheese filling. Perfect for a weeknight or special occasion dinner, this dish is sure to be a crowd pleaser!
Serving: 4
Prep Time: 15 minutes
Ready Time: 45 minutes

Ingredients:

- 2 medium yellow squash or zucchini
- 2 tablespoons olive oil
- 2 cloves garlic, minced
- 3 strips bacon, cut into small pieces
- 3/4 cup frozen peas
- 2 eggs
- 1/2 cup grated parmesan cheese
- 1/4 cup chopped parsley
- Salt and pepper, to taste

Instructions:
1. Preheat the oven to 350°F.
2. Cut the squash lengthwise and place on a baking sheet. Drizzle with olive oil and bake for 25 minutes.
3. Heat a large skillet over medium heat and add the bacon pieces. Cook until crispy.
4. Add the minced garlic and cook for 1 minute.
5. Add the frozen peas and cook for 3-4 minutes until heated through.
6. In a medium bowl, whisk together the eggs, parmesan cheese, parsley, salt, and pepper.
7. Remove the squash from the oven and fill each with the bacon pea mixture.
8. Pour the egg mixture over the squash and bake for an additional 20 minutes.
9. Serve warm.

Nutrition Information:
- 245 calories
- 15 g fat
- 10 g carbohydrates
- 17 g protein

36. Carbonara Stuffed Artichokes

Carbonara Stuffed Artichokes are a flavorful and satisfying way to enjoy artichokes for lunch or dinner. Made with cheese, garlic, herbs, and spices, these artichokes packs an intense flavor in every bite.
Serving: 4-6

Preparation Time: 15 minutes
Ready Time: 45 minutes

Ingredients:
-4 artichokes
-2 cloves garlic, minced
-1 cup shredded parmesan
-1 cup heavy cream
-1 tablespoon olive oil
-1 teaspoon thyme
-1 teaspoon oregano
-1 teaspoon red pepper flakes
-Salt and pepper to taste

Instructions:
1. Preheat oven to 375 degrees.
2. Cut the stems off of the artichokes and remove the tough outer leaves.
3. In a bowl, mix together the garlic, cheese, heavy cream, olive oil, thyme, oregano, and red pepper flakes.
4. Stuff the artichokes with the cheese mixture, then place the artichokes in a baking dish.
5. Drizzle with olive oil and season with salt and pepper.
6. Bake for 40-45 minutes, or until artichokes are tender.

Nutrition Information:
Serving Size: 1 artichoke
Calories: 214
Total Fat: 19g
Saturated Fat: 9g
Cholesterol: 55mg
Sodium: 309mg
Total Carbohydrates: 11g
Dietary Fiber: 5g
Sugars: 2g
Protein: 8g

37. Carbonara Stuffed Chicken Breasts

Carbonara Stuffed Chicken Breasts are a cheesy and flavorful dish that will delight the whole family! Filled with a bacon and Parmesan cream sauce, they are sure to be a hit for dinner.
Serving:
Makes 4 servings.
Preparation Time:
20 minutes
Ready Time:
40 minutes

Ingredients:
- 4 boneless, skinless chicken breasts
- 4 slices of bacon, chopped
- 1/2 cup Parmesan cheese, grated
- 1/3 cup heavy cream
- 2 tablespoons oil
- Salt and pepper to taste

Instructions:
1. Preheat oven to 350°F
2. Pound chicken breasts to even thickness
3. Heat oil in a skillet over medium-high heat and add bacon.Cook for about 10 minutes, stirring occasionally, until bacon is cooked through
4. Remove bacon from heat and spoon into the chicken breasts, pressing to secure the filling
5. Place chicken breasts in a greased baking dish and sprinkle with Parmesan cheese and salt and pepper.
6. Pour heavy cream over the top and cover with foil
7. Bake for 30 to 40 minutes, or until chicken is cooked through

Nutrition Information:
Per Serving (1 chicken breast): Calories: 436, Fat: 23.3g, Saturated Fat: 9.7g, Carbohydrates: 2.4g, Protein: 47.8g

38. Carbonara Stuffed Pork Chops

Carbonara Stuffed Pork Chops are a classic Italian-inspired dish. These easy-to-make pork chops are filled with a creamy Italian-style carbonara sauce, making them perfect for a hearty, delicious dinner.

Serving:

Makes 4 servings.

Preparation Time:

15 minutes.

Ready Time:

45 minutes.

Ingredients:

4 (4-ounce) bone-in pork chops

1 teaspoon garlic powder

1 teaspoon onion powder

1 teaspoon dried oregano

1 teaspoon dried basil

4 tablespoons butter

4 ounces bacon, cooked and crumbled

3 scallions, white and green parts chopped

4 ounces Parmesan cheese, grated

½ cup low-sodium chicken broth

Salt and pepper to taste

Instructions:

1. Preheat oven to 375 degrees F.

2. Sprinkle pork chops with garlic powder, onion powder, oregano and basil.

3. Heat butter in a large oven-proof skillet over medium-high heat. Brown pork chops on both sides and remove from heat.

4. In a medium bowl, combine bacon, scallions, Parmesan and chicken broth.

5. Place pork chops back in skillet and spoon carbonara mixture over the top.

6. Bake for 30-35 minutes or until pork chops are fully cooked through to an internal temperature of 145 degrees F.

7. Serve and enjoy!

Nutrition Information:

Per serving: 347 calories; 19.7 g fat; 4.9 g carbohydrates; 30.6 g protein; 35 mg cholesterol; 644 mg sodium.

39. Carbonara Stuffed Beef Tenderloin

Carbonara Stuffed Beef Tenderloin is an elegant and delicious meal perfect for a special dinner. This dish features a beef tenderloin filled with a combination of bacon, onion, garlic, a creamy carbonara sauce, and thyme. Serve this savory tenderloin with some roasted vegetables for a hearty and enjoyable meal.
Serving: 4
Prep Time: 20 mins
Cook Time: 30 mins

Ingredients:
- 2 lbs beef tenderloin
- 3 slices bacon, chopped
- 1 small onion, chopped
- 3 cloves garlic, minced
- 2 Tablespoons olive oil
- 1/2 cup parmesan cheese
- 1/2 cup cream
- 1 teaspoon dried thyme
- Salt and pepper, to taste

Instructions:
1. Preheat oven to 375°F.
2. In a large skillet, heat olive oil over medium-high heat. Add bacon, onion, and garlic and sauté until bacon is crisp.
3. In a separate bowl, mix together the parmesan cheese, cream, thyme, salt, and pepper.
4. Place the beef tenderloin on a cutting board and slice down the center, almost all the way through (but not completely).
5. Stuff the inside of the beef tenderloin with the bacon mixture.
6. Place the beef tenderloin in a baking dish, pour the cheese and cream mixture over it, and season with salt and pepper.
7. Cover the baking dish and bake in a preheated oven for 30 minutes.

Nutrition Information:

Calories: 588 kcal, Carbohydrates: 5 g, Protein: 30g, Fat: 44 g, Saturated
Fat: 17 g, Cholesterol: 110 mg, Sodium: 257 mg, Potassium: 540 mg,
Sugar: 1 g, Vitamin A: 187 IU, Vitamin C: 1 mg, Calcium: 164 mg, Iron:
3 mg

40. Carbonara Stuffed Veal Chops

Carbonara Stuffed Veal Chops is an Italian dish consisting of veal chops,
filled with bacon, parmesan cheese, and carbonara sauce. It is an
excellent meal for lunch or dinner, with a flavorful combination of pork,
cheese, and sauce.
Serving: 4
Preparation Time: 10 minutes
Ready Time: 30 minutes

Ingredients:
• 4 veal chops
• sea salt, black pepper, to taste
• 4 slices bacon
• 2 eggs
• 2 tablespoons grated parmesan cheese
• 2 tablespoons chopped parsley
• 1/4 cup of carbonara sauce

Instructions:
1. Preheat the oven to 350°F.
2. Sprinkle salt and black pepper on both sides of the veal chops.
3. In a pan cook the bacon until it is crispy.
4. In a small bowl, whisk together the eggs, parmesan cheese, chopped
parsley and carbonara sauce.
5. Place the veal chops on a baking dish and top each one with the bacon
and the egg mixture.
6. Bake in the oven for 25-30 minutes or until the veal chops are cooked
through.
7. Serve hot and enjoy.

Nutrition Information (per serving):
Calories: 494kcal

Protein: 33.3g
Fat: 35.2g
Carbohydrates: 0.4g

41. Carbonara Meatballs

Carbonara Meatballs are an Italian, classic comfort food. A delicious gravy-based dish of soft meatballs flavoured with pepper, garlic and Parmesan cheese, served over freshly cooked pasta. This is sure to be a hit with the whole family.
Serving: 6
Preparation Time: 10 minutes
Ready Time: 40 minutes

Ingredients:
- 500g minced beef
- 1 egg
- 1 teaspoon mixed dried herbs
- 2 cloves garlic
- 1 onion, diced
- 70g grated Parmesan cheese
- 160ml beef stock
- 4 tablespoons olive oil
- 120ml single cream
- 25g fresh parsley, chopped
- 2 tablespoons plain flour
- 400g of your favourite fresh pasta
- Salt and pepper to taste

Instructions:
1. Preheat the oven to 200°C.
2. In a large bowl, mix together the minced beef, egg, herbs, garlic, onion, Parmesan cheese and a little salt and pepper.
3. Roll the mixture into small balls and place on a lightly oiled baking sheet.
4. Put the baking sheet in the oven for 25-30 minutes, or until the meatballs are brown and cooked through.
5. In a large saucepan, heat the olive oil over a medium heat.

6. Add the beef stock and bring to the boil, then reduce the heat and simmer for 5 minutes.
7. Add cream, parsley, flour, salt and pepper and simmer for a further 5 minutes, stirring occasionally.
8. Add the cooked meatballs to the saucepan and simmer for 10 minutes.
9. Meanwhile, cook the pasta according to packet Instructions.
10. Serve the meatballs and sauce over the cooked pasta.

Nutrition Information (per serving):
Calories: 643, Fat: 28g, Cholesterol: 156mg, Sodium: 267mg, Carbohydrates: 57g, Protein: 35g

42. Carbonara Meatloaf

Carbonara meatloaf is a savory Italian-inspired meatloaf dish with a creamy carbonara-style sauce. The combination of smoky bacon, onions, garlic, Parmesan cheese, and eggs creates a delicious flavor profile that comes together perfectly in this easy to make dish.
Serving: 6
Preparation Time: 20 minutes
Ready Time: 1 hour

Ingredients:
- 1 ½ lbs ground beef
- 1 ½ cups breadcrumbs
- 4 slices bacon, finely chopped
- 1 onion, diced
- 2 cloves garlic, minced
- 2 eggs
- ½ cup Parmesan cheese
- 2 tablespoons olive oil
- 2 tablespoons flat leaf parsley, chopped
- Salt and pepper, to taste
- 2 cups marinara or tomato sauce

Instructions:
1. Preheat oven to 350°F.

2. In a large bowl, combine ground beef, breadcrumbs, bacon, onion, garlic, eggs, Parmesan cheese, olive oil, parsley, salt, and pepper, mixing until all Ingredients are evenly mixed.
3. Form the mixture into a loaf shape and place in a greased 9x13 inch baking dish.
4. Bake in preheated oven for 30 minutes.
5. Top meatloaf with marinara sauce and bake for an additional 30 minutes.
6. Allow to cool for 10 minutes before serving.

Nutrition Information:
Calories: 492 kcal
Carbohydrates: 24 g
Protein: 30 g
Fat: 27 g
Saturated Fat: 9.2 g
Cholesterol: 132 mg
Sodium: 913 mg
Potassium: 583 mg
Fiber: 2.4 g
Sugar: 2.5 g

43. Carbonara Burger

Carbonara Burger: Transform your classic Carbonara pasta into a burger with this delicious recipe!
Serving: 4
Preparation Time: 15 minutes
Ready Time: 15 minutes

Ingredients:
• 1 teaspoon olive oil
• 1/2 onion, finely diced
• 1/2 teaspoon garlic, minced
• 8 ounces ground beef
• Salt and pepper, to taste
• 4 hamburger buns
• 4 slices of bacon, cooked

- 1/2 cup mayonnaise
- 4 ounces Parmesan cheese, shredded
- 1/2 cup parsley, chopped
- 2 cups cooked white pasta

Instructions:
1. In a pan, heat the olive oil over medium-high heat and cook the onion and garlic until they are lightly browned, about 3 minutes.
2. Add in the ground beef and season with salt and pepper. Cook the beef until it is browned.
3. Toast the hamburger buns in the oven or on the stovetop.
4. In a bowl, mix the mayonnaise, parmesan cheese, parsley, bacon, and cooked white pasta.
5. Place the beef patties on the buns, then top with the carbonara mixture.

Nutrition Information:
Calories: 450 kcal,
Fat: 22.9 g,
Carbs: 33 g,
Protein: 25.6 g

44. Carbonara Hot Dogs

Carbonara Hot Dogs
Servings: 4
Preparation Time: 10 minutes
Ready Time: 25 minutes

Ingredients:
- 4 hot dogs
- 4 sheets of lasagna
- 1 cup of Parmesan cheese, grated
- 1/2 cup of bacon, diced
- 1/2 cup of peas
- 2 tablespoons of butter
- 2 cloves of garlic, minced
- 1 teaspoon of Italian seasoning

- Salt and pepper to taste

Instructions:
1. Preheat oven to 375 degrees Fahrenheit.
2. Cut each hot dog into 6 pieces, and then cut each slice of lasagna into 4 pieces.
3. In a large bowl, mix together the hot dogs, lasagna, Parmesan cheese, bacon, peas, butter, garlic, Italian seasoning, salt, and pepper to combine.
4. Spread the mixture onto a greased baking sheet and bake for 20-25 minutes, or until the edges of the lasagna are golden brown.
5. Serve warm and enjoy!

Nutrition Information: Each serving provides 305 calories, 24.2g of fat, 9.3g of carbohydrates, 4.2g of dietary fiber, 8.4g of protein, and 1.4g of sugar.

45. Carbonara Sausage

Carbonara Sausage is a classic Italian-inspired dish made with rich and creamy spaghetti, smoky Italian sausage, and a flavorful garlic and Parmesan cheese sauce. It's ready in less than 30 minutes and is sure to become a family favorite.
Serving: 4
Preparation Time: 10 minutes
Ready Time: 20 minutes

Ingredients:
- 8 ounces spaghetti
- 1 tablespoon olive oil
- 1/2 pound Italian sausage, casings removed
- 2 cloves garlic, minced
- 3 large eggs
- 1/2 cup freshly grated Parmesan cheese, plus extra for garnish
- 2 tablespoons chopped fresh parsley, plus extra for garnish
- Salt and freshly ground black pepper, to taste

Instructions:

1. Bring a large pot of salted water to a boil over medium-high heat. Add the spaghetti and cook according to package Instructions until al dente. Reserve about 1/2 cup of the cooked pasta water, then drain the pasta and set aside.

2. Heat the olive oil in a large skillet over medium-high heat. Add the sausage and cook, breaking it apart with a wooden spoon, until browned and cooked through, about 5 minutes. Add the garlic and cook until fragrant, about 1 minute. Drain off any excess oil.

3. In a small bowl, whisk together the eggs and Parmesan cheese until well blended.

4. Add the cooked pasta to the skillet with the sausage and garlic and stir to combine. Pour the egg and Parmesan mixture over the pasta and stir to combine. Add the reserved pasta water, if necessary, to help create a creamy sauce.

5. Cook, stirring constantly, until the sauce has thickened and coats the noodles, about 2 minutes. Remove from the heat and stir in the parsley, salt, and pepper.

6. Serve topped with extra Parmesan cheese and parsley, if desired.

Nutrition Information Per Serving: Calories 454, Total Fat 29.4 g, Saturated Fat 9.2 g, Cholesterol 196 mg, Sodium 558 mg, Carbohydrates 18.9 g, Fiber 1.6 g, Protein 25.9 g

46. Carbonara Jerky

Carbonara Jerky is an exciting combination of the classic Italian dish with modern American jerky. This delicious treat is sure to please all that try it and is the perfect snack for a movie night or party.

Serving: Makes 4 servings
Preparation Time: 10 minutes
Ready Time: 25 minutes

Ingredients:
- 8 ounces of your favorite Beef Jerky
- 2 tablespoons olive oil
- 4 ounces pancetta, diced
- 2 cloves garlic, minced
- 1 cup low-sodium chicken broth

- 2 tablespoons all-purpose flour
- 2 tablespoons Parmesan cheese
- 2 eggs
- 2 tablespoons of parsley, chopped
- Salt & pepper to taste

Instructions:
1. Preheat the oven to 350°F.
2. Place the jerky on a baking sheet and bake for 10 minutes.
3. Meanwhile, heat the olive oil in a skillet over medium heat.
4. Add the pancetta and garlic and cook until lightly browned.
5. Add the chicken broth and bring to a simmer.
6. Whisk in the flour, stirring until the mixture thickens.
7. Remove from the heat and stir in the Parmesan cheese.
8. In a separate bowl, whisk together the eggs and parsley.
9. Gradually add the egg mixture to the skillet, stirring constantly.
10. Once the jerky is cooked, remove from the oven and let cool.
11. Break into small pieces and add to the skillet, stirring until everything is evenly coated.
12. Season with salt and pepper, if desired.
13. Divide between four plates and serve warm.

Nutrition Information:
Per Serving: Calories: 441
Fat: 27.2g
Saturated Fat: 5.6g
Cholesterol: 83mg
Sodium: 1,080mg
Carbohydrates: 27.6g
Fiber: 3.3g
Sugar: 9.2g
Protein: 17.3g

47. Carbonara Omelette

Carbonara Omelette is a traditional Italian dish based on eggs, shredded cheese, and bacon. It's simple yet delicious, and makes the perfect breakfast or dinner.

Serving: Makes 1 omelette
Preparation time: 5 minutes
Ready time: 10 minutes

Ingredients:
- 2 eggs
- 2 tablespoons cream
- 1 teaspoon Italian herbs
- 1 tablespoon butter
- 3 slices bacon, cooked and chopped
- ½ cup shredded Italian cheese (mozzarella, provolone, Parmesan, or a combination)
- ¼ teaspoon black pepper
- Salt, to taste

Instructions:
1. In a medium bowl, whisk together the eggs, cream, Italian herbs, and black pepper.
2. Heat the butter in a non-stick skillet over medium heat.
3. Add the eggs and cook until just set.
4. Sprinkle the cheese and bacon on one side and fold the other side over to make an omelette.
5. Cook until the cheese is melted and the omelette is golden brown.
6. Serve immediately.

Nutrition Information (per serving):
Calories: 370, Fat: 25g, Carbohydrates: 1g, Protein: 28g, Sodium: 390mg, Cholesterol: 160mg

48. Carbonara Quiche

Carbonara Quiche is a favorite Italian-style dish made with eggs, bacon, Parmesan cheese, and cream. This quiche is an easy dish for a busy weeknight dinner, and it also makes a delicious brunch dish.
Serving: 6-8
Preparation Time: 10 minutes
Ready Time: 45 minutes

Ingredients:
- 3-4 slices of bacon, cut into 1 cm cubes
- 6 eggs
- 1/4 cup grated Parmesan cheese
- 1/2 cup heavy cream
- 1/4 teaspoon freshly ground black pepper
- 1 9-inch unbaked pastry shell

Instructions:
1. Preheat the oven to 375°F (190°C).
2. Place the bacon cubes in a large skillet over medium high heat. Cook, stirring often, until the bacon is crisp, about 5-7 minutes. Drain the cooked bacon pieces on paper towels and set aside.
3. In a bowl, whisk together the eggs, Parmesan, cream, and pepper until smooth.
4. Place the unbaked pastry shell in a 9-inch pie pan. Sprinkle the bacon over the bottom of the pie shell. Pour the egg mixture on top of the bacon.
5. Bake the quiche in the preheated oven for 25-30 minutes, until the top is golden brown and the center is set.
6. Let the quiche cool for at least 10 minutes before serving.

Nutrition Information:
Serving size 1/8 of quiche
Calories 340, Fat 27g, Cholesterol 185mg, Sodium 271mg, Carbohydrates 14g, Protein 10g.

49. Carbonara Frittata

This Carbonara Frittata is a comforting Italian-inspired dish with zesty flavors and cheesy goodness. It is filling, yet light enough for any meal, and is great served with a side salad or a warm slice of garlic bread.
Serving: 6-8
Preparation Time: 10 minutes
Ready Time: 20 minutes

Ingredients:
- 6 eggs, beaten

- 3/4 cup cream
- 1/2 cup parmesan cheese, grated
- 3 pieces of bacon, chopped
- 2 cloves garlic, chopped
- 3 tbsp Italian parsley, chopped
- 2 handfuls fresh baby spinach leaves
- Salt & pepper, to taste

Instructions:
1. Preheat oven to 350°F.
2. In a large bowl, whisk together eggs, cream, parmesan cheese, bacon, garlic, parsley, and salt & pepper until all Ingredients are combined.
3. Heat a large oven-safe skillet over medium-high heat. Add spinach leaves and cook until wilted, about 2 minutes.
4. Pour the egg mixture into the skillet and mix with the spinach.
5. Reduce the heat to low and cook for 10 minutes or until eggs are mostly set.
6. Transfer skillet to the preheated oven and bake for 10 minutes, or until edges of frittata are set.
7. Allow the frittata to cool before serving.

Nutrition Information: Per Serving (1/6 of frittata): 339 calories; 22.8g fat; 10.6g saturated fat; 16.1g carbohydrates; 4.1g sugar; 13.9g protein

50. Carbonara Scramble

Carbonara Scramble is an incredibly easy and extremely tasty brunch dish. With just a few Ingredients and a few minutes of work, you can have a delicious cooked breakfast ready to serve.
Serving: Serves 2
Preparation Time: 10 minutes
Ready Time: 10 minutes

Ingredients:
• 3 large eggs
• 2 tablespoons butter
• 2 tablespoons grated Parmesan cheese

- 2 tablespoons heavy cream
- 1/2 teaspoon chopped fresh Parsley
- 2 slices of cooked bacon, crumbled
- Salt and Pepper, to taste

Instructions:
1. Beat the eggs in a bowl until fluffy and slightly pale.
2. Heat the butter in a non-stick pan over medium-high heat.
3. Add the beaten eggs to the pan and cook, stirring occasionally, until the eggs are scrambled.
4. Reduce the heat to low and add the Parmesan cheese, cream, bacon, parsley, salt, and pepper.
5. Continue stirring and cooking until the cheese is melted and the eggs are cooked to your desired consistency.
6. Serve your Carbonara Scramble with toast or hash browns, and enjoy!

Nutrition Information: Each serving contains 208 calories, 17 g fat, 4.2 g carbohydrates, 10.3 g protein.

51. Carbonara Benedict

Carbonara Benedict is an Italian-inspired breakfast dish that combines eggs, pancetta and carbonara sauce with a fried poached egg. It's perfect for a weekend brunch.
Serving: 4
Preparation time: 15 minutes
Ready time: 40 minutes

Ingredients:
- 8-ounces of pancetta, diced
- 2 tablespoons of olive oil
- 4 large eggs
- 4 slices of Italian bread
- 2 tablespoons of butter
- ¼ cup of parsley, chopped
- ¼ cup of fresh basil, chopped
- ½ cup of carbonara sauce
- ¼ teaspoon of ground black pepper

Instructions:
1. Preheat the oven to 350 degrees Fahrenheit and grease 4 individual ramekins.
2. Heat a skillet or saucepan over medium-high heat and add the diced pancetta. Cook for 5 minutes, stirring frequently.
3. In the meantime, in a medium bowl mix together the olive oil, eggs, parsley, and basil.
4. Divide the egg mixture into the 4 ramekins and bake in the preheated oven for 15 minutes.
5. Meanwhile, melt the butter in a large skillet over medium-low heat.
6. Add the Italian bread slices and cook for 2-3 minutes per side until toasted.
7. To assemble the Carbonara Benedict, layer one slice of toasted Italian bread in a shallow bowl and top it with a poached egg.
8. Spoon the carbonara sauce over the egg.
9. Remove the egg cups from the oven and top each slice of bread with an egg cup.
10. Garnish with the cooked pancetta and remaining parsley and basil.

Nutrition Information (per serving): Calories 280, fat 19 g, protein 15 g, carbohydrates 10 g, fiber 2 g, sugar 2 g, sodium 440 mg.

52. Carbonara Casserole

Carbonara Casserole is a delicious and comforting meal of pasta and creamy sauce with bacon. It's a rich and creamy dish that's perfect for feeding the whole family, and can be easily thrown together in under an hour.
Serving: 6
Preparation Time: 15 minutes
Ready Time: 45 minutes

Ingredients:
- 1 lb rigatoni pasta
- 4 slices bacon, cooked and crumbled
- 1/2 cup onion, diced
- 2 cloves garlic, minced

- 2 cups heavy cream
- 1/2 cup Parmesan cheese, plus more for topping
- 1 teaspoon Italian seasoning
- Salt and pepper, to taste

Instructions:
1. Preheat oven to 350°F.
2. Bring a large pot of salted water to a boil, and cook the pasta for two minutes less than recommended (it should be slightly underdone). Drain and set aside.
3. Heat a large skillet over medium heat, and add the bacon. Cook, stirring occasionally, until the bacon is crisp and golden. Remove the bacon with a slotted spoon and drain on a plate.
4. Pour off all but 2 tablespoons of the bacon fat from the skillet, and add the onion. Cook until the onion is softened and translucent, about 5 minutes.
5. Add the garlic and cook for another minute.
6. Pour in the cream and add the Parmesan cheese, Italian seasoning, salt, and pepper. Simmer the sauce for about 10 minutes until it has thickened slightly.
7. Add the bacon back to the skillet and stir to combine.
8. Put the rigatoni in an 8x8-inch baking dish and pour the cream sauce over top. Sprinkle with additional Parmesan cheese and bake in the preheated oven for 25 minutes.

Nutrition Information: (per serving)
Calories: 543
Fat: 35g
Carbohydrates: 32g
Protein: 20g

53. Carbonara Pie

Carbonara Pie is an Italian delicacy with a crispy pastry encasing a creamy and delicious carbonara filling. This dish is sure to impress any guest or family member at any dinner or brunch.
Serving: 6-8
Preparation Time: 20-25 minutes

Ready Time: 1 hour

Ingredients:
- 2 sheets of pre-made frozen puff pastry
- 8 slices of bacon
- 2 tablespoons of finely chopped parsley
- 100 g grated parmesan cheese
- 4 whole eggs, lightly beaten
- 100 ml of cream
- 80 g of pecorino cheese, grated
- Salt and pepper to taste

Instructions:
1. Preheat the oven to 200°C and line a baking tray with parchment paper.
2. Cut the bacon into small cubes and fry them in a hot pan for 5 minutes. Remove from heat and let it cool down completely.
3. On a flat surface, lay one sheet of puff pastry and spread over it a mixture of parsley, bacon, parmesan, pecorino cheese and season with salt and pepper.
4. Place the other sheet of pastry on top and press the edges together to close the pie.
5. With a fork, make several holes on the surface of the pastry and spread the beaten eggs evenly.
6. Bake the Carbonara Pie in the oven for 25 minutes or until golden brown.
7. Let the Carbonara Pie cool down for 15 minutes before serving.

Nutrition Information: Calories: 400, Fat: 24g, Protein: 14g, Carbs: 28g, Sodium: 670mg.

54. Carbonara Tart

Carbonara Tart is a savory tart with a crispy, buttery crust that is filled with creamy carbonara sauce and wonderfully melty cheese. It is a delicious meal that can be served as a main dish for dinner or a side dish for lunch.
Serving: 8

Preparation Time: 15 minutes
Ready Time: 45 minutes

Ingredients:
- 1/2 package of ready-made tart dough
- 2 tablespoons olive oil
- 1 onion, chopped
- 8 slices bacon, diced
- 3 eggs
- 2 cups heavy cream
- 1 cup grated Parmesan cheese
- Salt and pepper to taste

Instructions:
1. Preheat oven to 375 degrees
2. Grease a deep dish tart pan and line with dough.
3. Heat a skillet over medium-high heat and add olive oil. Sauté onion and bacon until the bacon is cooked and the onions are softened.
4. In a separate bowl, whisk together eggs, cream, Parmesan cheese, salt, and pepper.
5. Spoon the bacon-onion mixture into the tart pan.
6. Pour the egg mixture over the bacon-onion mixture and spread it evenly.
7. Bake the tart in the preheated oven for 30-35 minutes, or until the middle is set.
8. Let cool before slicing and serving.

Nutrition Information (per serving): 496 calories, 32g fat, 5g saturated fat, 372mg cholesterol, 677mg sodium, 33g carbohydrates, 2g fiber, 11g sugars, and 19g protein.

55. Carbonara Lasagna Rolls

Carbonara Lasagna Rolls are delicious bites filled with traditional carbonara and cheese flavors. An easy and delicious Italian dish, these rolls are perfect for any dinner or gathering.
Serving: 8
Preparation Time: 30 minutes

Ready Time: 40 minutes

Ingredients:
-1 lb lasagna noodles
-1/2 lb bacon, diced
-1 clove garlic, minced
-1/2 cup heavy cream
-2 cups mozzarella cheese, shredded
-2/3 cup Parmesan cheese, grated
-2 eggs
-1/2 tsp salt
-1/4 tsp black pepper

Instructions:
1. Preheat oven to 375 degrees F and lightly grease a 9x13 inch baking dish.
2. Cook lasagna noodles in boiling salted water according to package Instructions. Drain and set aside.
3. In a large skillet, cook bacon until crisp. Remove bacon from skillet and set aside.
4. Add garlic to skillet and cook until fragrant. Add heavy cream, mozzarella cheese, Parmesan cheese, eggs, salt and pepper. Cook until cheese is melted and mixture is creamy.
5. On a cutting board, layer lasagna noodles into 2 rows.
6. Spoon a heaping tablespoon of the cheese mixture onto each noodle and spread it evenly.
7. Place bacon bits over the cheese mixture.
8. Roll lasagna noodles and place the rolls into prepared baking dish.
9. Bake for 25 to 30 minutes, or until golden brown.

Nutrition Information:
Calories: 244kcal, Carbohydrates: 17.1g, Protein: 11.5g, Fat: 14.2g, Saturated Fat: 6.2g, Cholesterol: 78mg, Sodium: 581.0mg, Fiber: 0.3g, Sugar: 0.6g

56. Carbonara Lasagna Cups

Carbonara Lasagna Cups are a delicious and quite easy to prepare meal for dinner. This twist on the classic Carbonara, with layers of lasagna sheets, cheese, and your favorite sauce, make this a dish everyone will love.

Servings: 9
Preparation Time: 30 minutes
Ready Time: 45 minutes

Ingredients:
• 9 lasagna sheets
• 2 tablespoons olive oil
• 2 tablespoons butter
• 2 cloves garlic, minced
• 2 tablespoons all-purpose flour
• 2 cups low-fat milk
• 2 cups finely grated Parmesan cheese
• Salt and pepper to taste
• 2 tablespoons chopped fresh parsley
• 2 tablespoons finely chopped green onions
• 1/4 cup cooked bacon
• 2 cups shredded mozzarella cheese

Instructions:
1. Preheat oven to 350 degrees F.
2. Grease 9 medium-sized muffin cups with butter.
3. Put 1 lasagna sheet into each muffin cup, pressing down lightly to flatten.
4. Heat olive oil and butter in a large skillet over medium heat. Add garlic and sauté for about 1 minute.
5. Whisk in flour and cook for another minute, stirring constantly.
6. Slowly add milk while stirring constantly until the sauce thickens.
7. Stir in Parmesan cheese, salt, and pepper.
8. Remove from heat and stir in parsley, green onion, and bacon.
9. Ladle the sauce into the lasagna cups and top with mozzarella cheese.
10. Bake for 25 minutes or until cheese is melted and bubbling.
11. Let cool for about 5-10 minutes before serving.

Nutrition Information: (Per serving)
Calories: 195 | Fat: 10g | Protein: 10g | Carbs: 16g | Fiber: 1g

57. Carbonara Ravioli

Carbonara ravioli is a delicious Italian recipe consisting of filled pasta that is cooked and combined with cream, prosciutto, bacon, and grated Parmesan cheese. It is a rich and flavorful dish that is sure to satisfy even the pickiest of eaters.

Serving: 4-6
Preparation time: 20 minutes
Ready time: 25 minutes

Ingredients:
- 1 package of ravioli
- 4 tablespoons of extra-virgin olive oil
- 3 strips of bacon, chopped
- 4 ounces of prosciutto, chopped
- 2 cloves of garlic, minced
- 1/4 cup of white wine
- 1/2 cup of heavy cream
- 1/4 cup of grated Parmesan cheese
- Salt and pepper to taste

Instructions:
1. Bring a large pot of salted water to a boil, then add the ravioli and cook according to package Instructions.
2. Heat the olive oil in a large saucepan over medium heat. Add the chopped bacon and prosciutto and cook until crisp.
3. Add the garlic and white wine to the pan and remove from heat.
4. When the ravioli is done, carefully drain the water and add the ravioli to the saucepan, combining it with the bacon and prosciutto.
5. Turn the heat to low and add the heavy cream, Parmesan cheese, and season with salt and pepper to taste. Stir until the Parmesan cheese is melted and the sauce is thick and creamy.
6. Serve the Carbonara Ravioli hot and enjoy!

Nutrition Information: Per serving (1/6 of the recipe): Calories: 299, Fat: 16.2 g, Cholesterol: 53 mg, Sodium: 634 mg, Carbohydrates: 26.9 g, Fiber: 0.7 g, Protein: 9.8 g.

58. Carbonara Tortellini

Carbonara Tortellini is a creamy Italian pasta dish filled with bacon and cheese. This recipe is perfect for a quick weeknight dinner and can be made in 30 minutes or less.
Serving: 4
Preparation Time: 5 minutes
Ready Time: 25 minutes

Ingredients:
- 8 ounces uncooked cheese tortellini
- 4 slices bacon, diced
- 1 1/2 cups heavy cream
- 1/2 cup Parmesan cheese, grated
- 2 tablespoons butter
- Salt and freshly ground black pepper, to taste
- Chopped fresh parsley leaves, for garnishing (optional)

Instructions:
1. Cook the tortellini according to the package Instructions. Drain and set aside
2. Heat a large skillet over medium heat. Add the bacon and cook until golden and crisp. Transfer the bacon to a paper towel-lined plate to drain the excess fat, reserving 2 tablespoons of bacon fat in the skillet.
3. Add the butter and heavy cream to the reserved bacon fat in the skillet and stir until the butter has melted.
4. Add the Parmesan cheese, stirring until melted.
5. Add the cooked tortellini to the sauce and gently stir to combine. Season with salt and pepper, to taste.
6. Serve the Carbonara Tortellini sprinkled with bacon and parsley, if desired.

Nutrition Information:
Calories: 426 kcal, Carbohydrates: 20.3 g, Protein: 15.7 g, Fat: 30.1 g, Saturated Fat: 16 g, Polyunsaturated Fat: 1 g, Monounsaturated Fat: 9.4 g, Cholesterol: 94 mg, Sodium: 515 mg, Potassium: 380 mg, Sugar: 2.3 g

59. Carbonara Agnolotti

Carbonara Agnolotti is a delicious Italian dish that combines the classic carbonara flavors of eggs, bacon, and cheese in a delectable pasta dish. This dish is simple to make and packed full of flavor.
Serving: 4
Preparation Time: 10 minutes
Ready Time: 20 minutes

Ingredients:
- 1 package of carbonara agnolotti
- ½ cup of cubed bacon
- 2 eggs
- 1 tablespoon olive oil
- 1 tablespoon chopped parsley
- 2 cloves of garlic, minced
- 8 ounces of grated parmesan cheese
- Salt and pepper, to taste

Instructions:
1. Bring a large pot of salted water to a boil. Add the carbonara agnolotti and cook according to the Instructions on the package, usually 8-10 minutes.
2. Meanwhile, in a large skillet, cook the cubed bacon over medium heat. Cook until the bacon is lightly brown and crispy. Remove the bacon from the skillet and set aside.
3. In a small bowl, whisk together the eggs and Parmesan cheese, season with salt and pepper.
4. Once the agnolotti is cooked to al dente, drain and transfer them to the skillet with the bacon fat.
5. Add the olive oil and garlic and cook for 2-3 minutes.
6. Pour the egg and cheese mixture into the skillet, stirring until the sauce has thickened.
7. Add the cooked agnolotti and bacon to the skillet and stir to combine.
8. Garnish with parsley and serve.

Nutrition Information:
Calories: 399 kcal, Carbohydrates: 28.6 g, Protein: 22.7 g, Fat: 20.8 g, Saturated Fat: 7.9 g, Cholesterol: 152 mg, Sodium: 1200 mg, Potassium: 202 mg, Fiber: 2.2 g, Sugar: 2.7 g, Calcium: 306mg, Iron: 2mg.

60. Carbonara Gnocchi Casserole

Carbonara Gnocchi Casserole is an easy, yet delicious pasta dish that combines bacon, peas, and of course, gnocchi. It's a great weeknight dinner option sure to please all family members!

Serving: 8
Preparation Time: 15 minutes
Ready Time: 25 minutes

Ingredients:
- 1 package (16 ounces) potato gnocchi
- 1/2 cup diced bacon
- 1/2 cup frozen peas
- 2 cloves garlic, minced
- 2 teaspoon Italian seasoning
- Freshly ground black pepper (to taste)
- 2 cups heavy cream
- 1/2 cup grated Parmesan cheese
- Salt (to taste)

Instructions:
1. Preheat the oven to 375° F.
2. In a large skillet, cook the bacon over medium-high heat until crispy.
3. Remove the bacon from the skillet and set aside.
4. In the same skillet, add the gnocchi, peas, garlic, and Italian seasoning. Cook for 3 minutes, stirring often.
5. Add the heavy cream, and cook for an additional 5 minutes, stirring occasionally.
6. Remove from heat, and stir in the Parmesan cheese, salt, and pepper.
7. Transfer the mixture into a 9x13 inch baking dish.
8. Top with the bacon and bake for 20 minutes.
9. Serve hot.

Nutrition Information:
Serving size: 1/8 of the casserole
Calories: 484
Fat: 30g

Carbohydrates: 36g
Protein: 14g

61. Carbonara Spinach Dip

This Carbonara Spinach Dip is a delicious, cheesy way to get your greens.
It's easy to make and perfect for a cosy night in or entertaining family
and friends.
Serving:
This Carbonara Spinach Dip serves 8-10 people.
Preparation Time:
This Carbonara Spinach Dip takes 15 minutes to prepare.
Ready Time:
This Carbonara Spinach Dip takes 30 minutes to cook.

Ingredients:
8 ounces cream cheese
1/4 cup heavy cream
1/4 cup shredded Parmesan cheese
3 cloves garlic, minced
2 teaspoons Italian seasoning
1/2 teaspoon sea salt
1/4 teaspoon ground black pepper
1 1/2 cups cooked and drained spinach

Instructions:
1. Preheat oven to 350°F and grease a baking dish with nonstick cooking
spray.
2. In a medium bowl, combine cream cheese, heavy cream, Parmesan
cheese, garlic, Italian seasoning, salt, and pepper.
3. Add the spinach and mix together until combined.
4. Transfer the mixture to the prepared baking dish and bake for 25-30
minutes.
5. Then turn on the broiler and cook for an additional 5 minutes, or until
golden and bubbly.

Nutrition Information:

This Carbonara Spinach Dip is packed with essential nutrients with an approximate 145 calories per serving, 10.7 g of fat, 4.5 g of carbohydrates, and 6.2 g of protein.

62. Carbonara Spinach Salad

Carbonara Spinach Salad is an Italian-style salad filled with delicious flavors. It's a perfect side dish for a summer cookout and is sure to be a huge crowd pleaser.
Serving: Serves 6.
Preparation Time: 10 minutes.
Ready Time: 15 minutes.

Ingredients:
• 6 cups of fresh spinach
• 2 tablespoons olive oil
• 2 tablespoons of Italian seasoning
• 1/4 cup parmesan cheese
• 4 cloves garlic, minced
• 4 slices bacon, cooked and crumbled
• 1/4 cup cooked and crumbled pancetta
• Salt and pepper to taste

Instructions:
1. In a large bowl, combine the spinach, olive oil, Italian seasoning, cheese, garlic, bacon, and pancetta.
2. Mix until all Ingredients are well combined.
3. Season with salt and pepper.
4. Serve chilled.

Nutrition Information:
Calories 164, Total Fat 11.4g, Carbohydrates 4.2g, Protein 13g, Cholesterol 30mg, Sodium 271mg, Potassium 360 mg, Fiber 2.2g.

63. Carbonara Caprese Salad

Carbonara Caprese Salad is a delicious Italian-inspired dish featuring savory bacon, fragrant basil, and creamy mozzarella cheese.
Serving: 4 servings
Preparation Time: 15 minutes
Ready Time: 15 minutes

Ingredients:
- 4 slices bacon
- 1 lb. small campanelle pasta
- 4 cloves garlic
- 2 cups chopped fresh basil
- 2 cups cherry tomatoes, halved
- 1 cup cubed fresh mozzarella
- 2 tablespoons olive oil
- Salt and pepper, to taste

Instructions:
1. Cook the bacon in a large skillet over medium heat until crisp, about 8 minutes. Set aside to cool. Once cool, chop into small pieces.
2. Bring a large pot of salted water to a boil. Add the pasta and cook according to package Instructions until al dente. Drain and transfer to a large bowl.
3. Meanwhile, mince the garlic and add it to the bowl with the basil, tomatoes, and mozzarella. Add the chopped bacon pieces and drizzle the olive oil over top.
4. Gently toss the salad together until all of the Ingredients are combined. Season with salt and pepper, to taste. Serve immediately.

Nutrition Information: per serving (4 servings): Calories: 368, Fat: 14g, Saturated Fat: 5g, Cholesterol: 35mg, Sodium: 168mg, Carbohydrates: 44g, Fiber: 3g, Sugar: 2g, Protein: 13g.

64. Carbonara Antipasto Salad

Carbonara Antipasto Salad: This classic antipasto salad combines the delicious flavors of creamy, cheesy carbonara with a variety of fresh vegetables. A great choice for any summer gathering or meal, this Carbonara Antipasto Salad is sure to be a hit!

Serving: 4-6
Preparation time: 10 minutes
Ready time: 10 minutes

Ingredients:
- 1 (1 pound) package cubed cooked ham
- 2 cups cubed cooked bacon
- 4 cups cooked and drained pasta
- 1 cup Italian salad dressing
- 2 cups chopped tomatoes
- 2 cups halved black olives
- 2 cups diced mozzarella cheese
- 2 tablespoons grated Parmesan cheese

Instructions:
1. In a large bowl, combine ham, bacon, pasta, salad dressing, tomatoes, olives, cheese, and Parmesan cheese.
2. Mix until Ingredients are evenly incorporated.
3. Serve chilled.

Nutrition Information: Per Serving: 360 calories; 18.6 g fat; 22.7 g carbohydrates; 23.4 g protein

65. Carbonara Bruschetta Salad

This Carbonara Bruschetta Salad is the perfect way to enjoy all the flavors of spaghetti carbonara in a light and refreshing salad!

Serving: Serves 4
Preparation Time: 10 minutes
Ready Time: 10 minutes

Ingredients:
• 8 slices of French baguette
• 8 slices of bacon
• 2 tablespoons olive oil
• 2 cloves of garlic
• 2 eggs

• 2/3 cup of Parmigiano Reggiano cheese
• 4 fresh tomatoes
• Salt and pepper to taste
• 2 tablespoons of fresh parsley

Instructions:
1. Preheat the oven to 200°C/400°F.
2. Cut the French baguette into 8 slices and brush them with the olive oil.
3. Put the slices of bread in the oven for 5 minutes until they are golden and toasted.
4. Meanwhile, in a frying pan, cook the bacon until golden and crispy.
5. In a bowl, whisk the eggs, the Parmigiano Reggiano cheese and the crushed garlic cloves.
6. Cut the tomatoes in small cubes and place them in a bowl with the fresh parsley.
7. Place the slices of toast on a plate.
8. Top them with the tomato and parsley mixture, the cooked bacon and the egg mixture.
9. Add some salt and pepper to taste and enjoy!

Nutrition Information: Per Serving: Calories: 530; Total Fat: 32g; Saturated Fat: 13g; Sodium: 791mg; Protein: 20g; Carbs: 37g; Sugar: 4g; Fiber: 3g.

66. Carbonara Caesar Salad

Carbonara Caesar Salad is a delicious dish that combines crispy romaine lettuce with salty bacon, savory parmesan cheese and a creamy and flavorful carbonara-style egg sauce. It's the perfect combination of Italian flavors and a unique twist on Caesar salad.
Serving: 4-6
Preparation Time: 10 minutes
Ready Time: 15 minutes

Ingredients:
-Romaine lettuce, 4 cups chopped
-Bacon, 6 slices cooked and crumbled

-Parmesan cheese, ¼ cup shredded
-Black pepper, to taste
-For the Carbonara sauce:
-Egg yolks, 2
-Heavy cream, ½ cup
-Garlic, 1 clove minced
-Parmesan cheese, ¼ cup shredded
-Lemon juice, 1 tablespoon

Instructions:
1. Start by making the Carbonara sauce. In a bowl, whisk together the egg yolks, heavy cream, garlic, Parmesan cheese, and lemon juice.
2. In a large salad bowl, combine the romaine lettuce, bacon, Parmesan cheese and black pepper.
3. Pour the Carbonara sauce over the salad and gently toss to combine.
4. Taste and adjust the seasoning, if needed.
5. Serve the Carbonara Caesar Salad immediately.

Nutrition Information: per serving: Calories: 209, Fat: 14 g, Protein: 10 g, Carbohydrates: 3 g, Sodium: 361 mg

67. Carbonara Focaccia

Carbonara Focaccia is a savory Italian flatbread dish made with rich and creamy flavors. It is named after the classic pasta dish, carbonara, as it is topped with a sauce made up of bacon, eggs, and cheese, like the popular Italian pasta carbonara. This Focaccia dish is easy to make and requires minimal effort to put together.
Serving: 4-6
Preparation Time: 10 minutes
Ready Time: 20 minutes

Ingredients:
- 2 focaccia breads
- 4 real bacon strips
- 1/3 cup of grated Parmesan cheese
- 2 eggs
- 1/3 cup of heavy cream

- Salt and pepper to taste

Instructions:
1. Preheat oven to 350 degrees Fahrenheit.
2. Place focaccia breads on a sheet pan and bake for 5 minutes.
3. Meanwhile, cook bacon in a skillet over medium heat for 5 minutes until crisp.
4. In a bowl, whisk together eggs, cream, Parmesan, and salt and pepper.
5. Spread egg mixture over cooked focaccia breads.
6. Top with bacon pieces and additional grated Parmesan cheese.
7. Bake for 15 minutes at 350 degrees Fahrenheit.
8. Serve warm.

Nutrition Information:
Calories: 420 Fat: 28g Carbohydrates: 23g Protein: 18g

68. Carbonara Grilled Cheese

Carbonara Grilled Cheese
Serving: 4
Preparation Time: 5 minutes
Ready Time: 15 minutes

Ingredients:
• 4 thick slices of Italian bread
• 2 tablespoons butter
• 4.5 ounces turkey or chicken bacon, cooked and chopped
• 1 cup cooked broccoli florets
• 4 ounces cream cheese
• 1/3 cup grated Parmesan cheese
• Salt and pepper, to taste
• 2 large eggs

Instructions:
1. Preheat your oven's broiler.
2. Spread butter to one side of each slice of bread. Place the bread, butter side down, onto the baking sheet on top of the aluminum foil.
3. Top the bread with the cooked bacon and broccoli.

4. In a small bowl, mix the cream cheese, Parmesan cheese, salt, and pepper. Spread evenly over the Ingredients on the bread.
5. Crack the two eggs over the top of each sandwich and spread out the egg whites.
6. Place the baking sheet in the oven and broil for 5 minutes.
7. Remove from the oven and flip each sandwich over (so the egg is on the bottom). Return to the oven and broil for another 5 minutes, or until the egg is cooked.

Nutrition Information (Per Serving):
Calories: 342, Fat: 16g, Carbs: 30g, Protein: 16g

69. Carbonara Quesadilla

Carbonara Quesadilla: Carbonara Quesadilla combines yummy cheese and bacon flavors with a crispy tortilla shell. It's perfect as a snack or as a meal for lunch or dinner.
Serving: 4
Preparation Time: 10 mins
Ready Time: 15 mins

Ingredients:
- 8 small flour tortillas
- 4 slices thick-cut bacon, cooked and crumbled
- 2 cups spaghetti sauce
- 2 cups shredded Mozzarella cheese
- 1/2 cup grated Parmesan cheese
- 2 tablespoons crumbled cooked bacon

Instructions:
1. Preheat a large skillet on medium heat.
2. Place a tortilla in the skillet and top with a layer of spaghetti sauce.
3. Sprinkle with a generous amount of Mozzarella and Parmesan cheese.
4. Top with crumbled bacon and another tortilla.
5. Cook until the bottom is golden and cheese is melted, about 5 minutes.
6. Carefully flip and cook for an additional 5 minutes.
7. Cut the quesadilla in wedges and serve.

Nutrition Information:
Calories:369, Fat: 16 g, Protein: 16 g, Carbohydrates: 30 g, Sodium: 1201 mg, Fiber: 2 g.

70. Carbonara Enchiladas

Carbonara Enchiladas
Serving: 5
Preparation Time: 15 minutes
Ready Time: 45 minutes

Ingredients:
- 2 tablespoons olive oil
- 1/2 medium white onion, finely chopped
- 2 cloves garlic, finely chopped
- 2 cups cooked chicken, finely chopped
- 4 jalapeños, finely chopped
- 2 cups shredded Monterey Jack cheese
- 4 ounces cream cheese, softened
- 1 cup fresh pico de gallo
- 10 flour tortillas
- 2 cups your favorite tomato enchilada sauce
- 2 tablespoons chopped fresh cilantro

Instructions:
1. Preheat oven to 375°F.
2. Heat olive oil in a large skillet over medium heat. Add onion and garlic and cook until softened, about 5 minutes. Add chicken and jalapeños and cook for another 5 minutes.
3. In a medium bowl, mix together the cheese, cream cheese, and pico de gallo.
4. Spoon a heaping tablespoon of the cheese mixture onto each tortilla and roll up to form a burrito. Place the burritos in an 9x13-inch baking dish.
5. Pour the enchilada sauce over the top of the burritos and sprinkle with the remaining cheese and cilantro.

6. Bake in preheated oven for 25-30 minutes or until cheese is melted and bubbly.

Nutrition Information:
Per serving: 349 calories, 18 g fat, 28 g carb, 13 g protein

71. Carbonara Tacos

Carbonara Tacos is a tasty and creative riff on the classic Italian Carbonara dish. Combining a few key Carbonara Ingredients into a Mexican-style taco, this dish is perfect for a weeknight family dinner.
Serving: 4
Preparation Time: 15 minutes
Ready Time: 30 minutes

Ingredients:
- 4 large hard-shell tacos
- 1/2 pound of bacon, diced
- 1/2 cup of heavy cream
- 1/2 cup of shredded Parmesan cheese
- 2 cloves of garlic, minced
- 1/2 onion, diced
- 1/4 teaspoon of red pepper flakes
- 1/2 teaspoon of ground black pepper
- 1/2 teaspoon of salt

Instructions:
1. Preheat an oven to 350°F and place the tacos in the oven for 10-12 minutes.
2. Heat a large skillet over medium heat. Add the bacon to the pan and cook until they are crispy.
3. Remove the bacon from the pan and set aside. To the same pan, add the garlic, onions, red pepper flakes, black pepper, and salt. Cook until the onions are soft and translucent.
4. Add the cream and parmesan cheese to the skillet and stir to combine.
5. Place the crisped bacon back into the skillet and cook until the cheese sauce thickens.

6. Remove from heat and spoon the carbonara mixture into the tacos shells.
7. Serve warm with your favorite taco toppings.

Nutrition Information: per serving, Calories: 387, Fat: 24g, Carbohydrates: 24g, Protein: 17g, Sodium: 803mg

72. Carbonara Burritos

Carbonara Burritos: These burritos filled with creamy carbonara pasta are a great twist on a classic Italian dish, perfect as a tasty dinner or lunch option.
Serving: 4
Preparation Time: 15 minutes
Ready Time: 10 minutes

Ingredients:
- 8 large flour tortillas
- 5 ounces cooked bacon, diced
- 1/4 cup diced onions
- 4 cloves garlic, minced
- 2 tablespoons olive oil
- 2 cups cooked penne
- 2 tablespoons butter
- 2 tablespoons heavy cream
- 1/2 cup grated parmesan cheese
- 1/2 teaspoon black pepper
- Salt, to taste

Instructions:
1. Preheat a skillet over medium-high heat.
2. Add the bacon, onions, and garlic. Sauté for 5 minutes.
3. Add the olive oil and penne and cook for another 5 minutes or until the penne is heated through.
4. Add the butter and stir until melted.
5. Add the heavy cream, parmesan cheese, and black pepper. Stir to combine.

6. Place equal amounts of the carbonara mix onto each tortilla and roll up into burrito.
7. Serve warm.

Nutrition Information: Per serving: 320 Calories, 19 g Fat, 7 g Protein, 25 g Carbohydrates

73. Carbonara Chimichangas

Carbonara Chimichangas are a unique twist on two beloved dishes - an Italian classic and Mexican staple. This dish brings the creaminess of carbonara with the crunchiness of a chimichanga. Serve as an appetizer or main dish!
Serving: 4-6
Preparation Time: 20 minutes
Ready Time: 40 minutes

Ingredients:
• 8 large flour tortillas
• 2 cups cooked cheese ravioli
• 3 cups of shredded cheese
• 4 slices of bacon, diced
• 1/4 cup of diced yellow onion
• 1/2 cup diced ham
• 6 cloves of garlic, minced
• 1/4 teaspoon of black pepper
• 2 eggs
• 2 cups of heavy cream

Instructions:
1. Preheat oven to 375°F.
2. In a large pan, cook the bacon until crispy. Remove the bacon and drain on a paper towel-lined plate. Reserve 2 tablespoons of bacon fat in the pan.
3. Add the onion, garlic, and ham to the pan and sauté for 5 minutes, until onions are softened.

4. In a small bowl, whisk together the eggs and heavy cream until smooth.
5. Place the tortillas on a work surface and spread 1/4 cup of the cooked ravioli on each one. Top with the bacon, onion mixture, and 1/2 cup of the shredded cheese.
6. Roll up the tortillas and secure with toothpicks.
7. Place the rolled up chimichangas in a lightly greased baking dish.
8. Pour the egg and cream mixture over the chimichangas.
9. Sprinkle the remaining shredded cheese over the top.
10. Bake for 20–25 minutes, until cheese is golden and bubbly.

Nutrition Information:
Calories: 707, Fat: 42.8g, Cholesterol: 110mg, Sodium: 845mg, Carbohydrates: 51.1g, Protein: 29.9g

74. Carbonara Taquitos

Carbonara Taquitos are a tasty appetizer or snack that combines the classic flavors of carbonara sauce with crunchy taquitos. They're easy to make and guaranteed to be a hit at any game day, get-together, or party.
Serving: 2
Preparation Time: 20 minutes
Ready Time: 50 minutes

Ingredients:
• 8 Taquitos
• 4 ounces carbonara creamy sauce
• 2 tablespoons grated Parmesan
• ½ teaspoon dried parsley
• 2 tablespoons butter

Instructions:
1. Preheat the oven to 350 degrees Fahrenheit.
2. Place the taquitos on a parchment-lined baking sheet.
3. In a mixing bowl, combine the carbonara creamy sauce, Parmesan, parsley, and butter.
4. Spread the creamy mixture on top of each taquito.
5. Bake for 35 minutes or until the taquitos are golden-brown.

6. Enjoy!

Nutrition Information:
Calories: 250
Fat: 15g
Protein: 5g
Carbohydrates: 16g
Sugar: 1g
Fiber: 1g

75. Carbonara Empanadas

Carbonara Empanadas are tasty turnovers made with a delicious combination of egg, cream, and Parmesan cheese for a delightful appetizer or snack.
Serving: 12 empanadas
Preparation Time: 30 minutes
Ready Time: 1 hour 15 minutes

Ingredients:
1 cup all-purpose flour
1 teaspoon salt
4 tablespoons cold unsalted butter
1 tablespoon olive oil
1/2 cup plus 2 tablespoons cold water
4 ounces bacon
2 cups grated Parmesan cheese
2 eggs
1/2 cup heavy cream

Instructions:
1. In a large bowl, combine the flour, salt, and butter. With your hands, mix until it resembles coarse meal.
Add the olive oil and cold water, and mix until the dough holds together. Form the dough into a ball and let it rest for 10 minutes.
2. Meanwhile, preheat the oven to 375°F. In a skillet, cook the bacon over medium heat until the bacon is crispy. Set aside on a plate lined with paper towel to cool.

3. In a bowl, mix together the Parmesan cheese, eggs, and heavy cream.
4. On a lightly floured surface, roll the dough to about 1/8-inch in thickness. Cut into 12 rounds using a 3-inch biscuit cutter.
5. Place a heaping tablespoon of the bacon and cheese filling in the center of each round. Fold over and press to seal with your fingers. Place on a baking sheet.
6. Brush the empanadas with the egg wash. Bake for 30 minutes, or until they are golden brown. Let cool before serving.

Nutrition Information(per empanada):
Calories: 255, Protein: 8g, Total Fat: 15g, Sodium: 231mg, Total Carbohydrates: 17g, Fiber: 1g

76. Carbonara Pierogies

Carbonara Pierogies are pillowy pockets of savory deliciousness filled with a cheesy bacon and egg filling. They're easy to prepare and make a wonderful side dish or meal.
Serving: 6
Preparation Time: 15 minutes
Ready Time: 20 minutes

Ingredients:
-12 frozen pierogies
-2 slices of bacon, diced
-1/4 cup finely diced yellow onion
-1/4 cup grated parmesan cheese
-1/4 cup milk
-2 large eggs
-2 tablespoons chopped parsley
-Salt and pepper to taste

Instructions:
1. Cook pierogies according to package directions.
2. In a medium skillet, cook the bacon and onion for about 5 minutes or until bacon is crisp and onions are softened.
3. In a medium bowl, whisk together parmesan cheese, milk, eggs, parsley, salt, and pepper.

4. Add cooked bacon and onion to the cheese mixture and mix until combined.
5. Add cooked pierogies to the cheese mixture and gently stir until well coated.
6. Grease an 8-inch square baking dish and spoon pierogies into dish.
7. Bake at 350°F for 15 minutes, or until the pierogies are heated through.

Nutrition Information (per serving):
Calories: 178, Fat: 8g, Saturated fat: 3g, Carbohydrates: 16g, Sugar: 1g, Protein: 7g, Sodium: 388mg, Cholesterol: 56mg.

77. Carbonara Potatoes

Carbonara Potatoes is an easy and comforting main dish, with a creamy texture and rich flavor.

SERVING: This dish serves 4 people.
PREPARATION TIME: 10 minutes
READY TIME: 25 minutes

Ingredients:
- 4 large potatoes, cut into cubes
- 4 cloves of garlic, chopped
- 1 cup of cream
- 1/2 cup of bacon, diced
- 1/2 cup of Parmesan cheese, grated
- 2 tablespoons of olive oil
- Salt and pepper to taste

Instructions:
1. Preheat oven to 375 degrees.
2. Place potato cubes on a baking sheet and season with salt and pepper.
3. Bake in the oven for 15 minutes.
4. Meanwhile, heat the oil in a skillet over medium heat.
5. Add garlic and cook for 1 minute.
6. Add bacon and cook until crisp.
7. Add cream and simmer for 5 minutes.

8. Add Parmesan cheese and stir until combined.

9. Add the potatoes to the skillet and stir until they are coated in the cheese sauce.

10. Serve and enjoy!

Nutrition Information: Per serving, this dish contains 346 calories, 21g fat, 5g saturated fat, 20g carbohydrates, 6.5g protein, and 1g fiber.

78. Carbonara Sweet Potatoes

Carbonara Sweet Potatoes is an easy and delicious recipe that packs a powerhouse of flavors. It is a great side dish to serve at any gathering or just to add some extra flavor to a typical weeknight dinner.

Serving: 4

Preparation Time: 15 minutes

Ready Time: 25 minutes

Ingredients:

-4 large sweet potatoes, peeled and cut into 1/2-inch cubes

-3 tablespoons olive oil

-2 cloves garlic, minced

-1/2 cup diced bacon

-1/2 teaspoon freshly ground black pepper

-3 tablespoons grated Parmesan cheese

-1 tablespoon chopped fresh parsley

Instructions:

1. Preheat oven to 375°F (190°C).

2. Place potatoes into a bowl and drizzle with oil.

3. Add garlic, bacon, black pepper, Parmesan cheese, and parsley; toss to combine.

4. Spread potatoes in an even layer on a baking sheet.

5. Bake in the preheated oven until potatoes are tender and lightly browned, about 25 minutes.

Nutrition Information:

Serving size: 1 (196g), Calories: 200, Carbs: 28g, Protein: 5g, Fat: 9g, Saturated fat: 2.5g, Sodium: 203mg, Cholesterol 8mg, Potassium: 515mg, Fiber: 4g, Sugar: 5g, Vitamin A: 12222 IU, Vitamin C: 10mg, Calcium: 54mg, Iron: 1.2mg.

79. Carbonara Mashed Potatoes

Carbonara Mashed Potatoes
Serving: 6
Preparation Time: 10 minutes
Ready Time: 25 minutes

Ingredients:
• 2 pounds potatoes, peeled and cubed
• 6 strips of bacon
• 2 tablespoons butter
• 1 cup heavy cream
• 2 cloves garlic, minced
• 1 teaspoon Kosher salt
• 1/2 teaspoon freshly ground black pepper
• 1 cup freshly grated Parmesan cheese
• 2 tablespoons chopped fresh parsley

Instructions:
1. Place the potatoes in a large pot and cover them with cold water.
2. Bring the water to a boil over medium-high heat and cook the potatoes for 10 to 12 minutes, until they are fork-tender.
3. While the potatoes are cooking, cook the bacon in a large skillet over medium heat until crisp. Remove bacon from the pan and drain it on paper towels; reserve 1 tablespoon of the bacon fat.
4. Drain the potatoes in a colander and return them to the pot.
5. Add the butter, cream, garlic, salt, and pepper to the pot and mash the potatoes until they are creamy.
6. Add the Parmesan cheese, parsley and bacon and mix everything together.
7. Add the reserved bacon fat and mix until everything is combined.

Nutrition Information:

Serving: One-sixth of the recipe, Calories: 228, Fat: 13g, Saturated Fat: 7g, Cholesterol: 36mg, Sodium: 366mg, Carbohydrates: 21g, Fiber: 2g, Sugar: 1g, Protein: 8g

80. Carbonara French Fries

Carbonara French Fries are a delicious twist on a classic Italian dish, with crispy potatoes, creamy carbonara sauce, and jalapeño slices! Served as a side or an appetizer, this dish is sure to be a hit!
Serving: 4
Preparation Time: 30 minutes
Ready Time: 30 minutes

Ingredients:
- Potatoes, 3-4 large
- Olive Oil, 2 tablespoons
- Carbonara Sauce, 2-3 tablespoons
- Jalapeño Peppers, sliced
- Parmesan Cheese, freshly grated
- Salt and Pepper to taste

Instructions:
1. Preheat oven to 350°F.
2. Peel and cut potatoes into wedges.
3. In a bowl, mix potato wedges with olive oil, salt, and pepper.
4. Arrange on a baking tray lined with parchment paper and bake for 25 minutes or until golden brown.
5. In the meantime, prepare the Carbonara sauce.
6. When potatoes are ready, transfer them to a plate and pour the Carbonara sauce over them.
7. Sprinkle with Parmesan cheese and jalapeños.

Nutrition Information:
Calories: 455, Fat: 19g, Saturated Fat: 3g, Cholesterol: 10mg, Sodium: 254mg, Carbohydrates: 58g, Fiber: 5g , Protein: 11g, Sugar: 4g.

81. Carbonara Onion Rings

Carbonara Onion Rings are a delicious appetizer made with onions, shredded cheese, bacon, and a traditional Italian Carbonara sauce. This savory snack will have your guests coming back for more!

Serving: 4-6
Preparation Time: 15 minutes
Ready Time: 35 minutes

Ingredients:
- 2 large onions, sliced into ½ inch rings
- ½ cup carbonara sauce
- 2 cups shredded cheese
- 2 ounces bacon bits
- Salt to taste

Instructions:
1. Preheat oven to 375°F.
2. In a small bowl, combine carbonara sauce, shredded cheese, and bacon bits.
3. Arrange onion rings on a baking sheet and sprinkle with salt.
4. Spread cheese mixture evenly over the onion rings.
5. Bake in preheated oven for 20 minutes or until onion rings have softened.

Nutrition Information:
Calories: 223, Fat: 11.7g, Saturated Fat: 5.2g, Cholesterol: 33mg, Sodium: 563mg, Carbohydrates: 16.7g, Fiber: 1.7g, Sugar: 2.6g, Protein: 12.3g.

82. Carbonara Croquettes

Carbonara Croquettes are delicious Italian-inspired potato croquettes filled with bacon, mozzarella and parmesan cheese. They are crunchy on the outside and creamy on the inside--the perfect combination for a delicious snack.

Serving: Makes 8 croquettes
Preparation Time: 10 minutes
Ready Time: 30 minutes

Ingredients:
- 2 Russet potatoes
- 2 large eggs
- 2 tbsp olive oil
- 2 cloves of garlic, minced
- 1/2 cup cooked bacon, diced
- 1/2 cup mozzarella cheese, shredded
- 1/2 cup Parmesan cheese, shredded
- Salt, to taste

Instructions:
1. Preheat oven to 375 degrees F.
2. Wash and peel the potatoes, then grate them.
3. Add the grated potatoes to a large bowl, then add in the eggs, olive oil, garlic, bacon, mozzarella cheese, parmesan cheese and salt. Mix together well.
4. Using your hands, shape the mixture into small croquette shaped form. Place them on a baking sheet lined with parchment paper.
5. Bake in preheated oven for 25-30 minutes, or until the croquettes are golden brown.

Nutrition Information: Per Serving (1 croquette): Calories 140; Fat 9.4g; Saturated Fat 3.2g; Cholesterol 48.2mg; Sodium 201.5mg; Carbohydrates 8.4g; Fiber 0.7g; Sugar 0.5g; Protein 5.6g

83. Carbonara Schnitzel

Carbonara Schnitzel
Serving: 4
Preparation time: 15 mins
Ready time: 40 mins

Ingredients:
- 4 (¼-inch-thick) slices pork loin or veal schnitzel
- 2 tablespoons olive oil
- 4 ounces bacon
- 3 cloves garlic, minced

- 2 cups heavy cream
- 1/2 cup freshly grated Parmesan, plus more for garnish
- 2 large eggs
- 2 tablespoons chopped fresh parsley
- Salt and freshly ground black pepper

Instructions:
1. Preheat oven to 350°F (175°C).
2. Heat the oil in a large skillet over medium-high heat. Add the schnitzel and cook until golden brown, about 5 minutes per side. Transfer to a baking sheet and bake for about 10-15 minutes, or until cooked through.
3. Meanwhile, cook the bacon in the same skillet over medium heat until lightly cooked, about 7 minutes. Stir in the garlic and cook for another minute. Reduce heat to low, then pour in cream and stir in the Parmesan cheese.
4. In a small bowl, whisk together the eggs and parsley. Slowly pour into the skillet while stirring constantly, until everything is combined and creamy.

Nutrition Information:
Per Serving: Calories: 377 kcal, Carbohydrates: 2 g, Protein: 18.4 g, Fat: 32 g, Saturated Fat: 15 g, Cholesterol: 147 mg, Sodium: 374 mg, Potassium: 254 mg, Sugar: 1 g, Vitamin A: 875 IU, Vitamin C: 1.3 mg, Calcium: 152 mg, Iron: 1.1 mg

84. Carbonara Tempura

Carbonara Tempura is a dish made from pasta, eggs, and cheese mixed with tempura batter and then deep fried. It makes for a tasty and savory treat, perfect for any meal or event.
Serving: 4
Preparation time: 10 minutes
Ready time: 20 minutes

Ingredients:
- 1 egg
- 1/4 cup Parmesan cheese, grated
- 1/4 cup Panko breadcrumbs

- 1/2 teaspoon garlic powder
- Pinch of Italian seasoning
- 2 cups cooked pasta (penne, elbows, or your favorite shape)
- Vegetable or peanut oil for frying
- Tempura batter (optional)

Instructions:
1. In a small bowl, whisk the egg with the Parmesan cheese, Panko breadcrumbs, garlic powder, and Italian seasoning.
2. Transfer the mixture into a large bowl and mix in the cooked pasta until evenly distributed.
3. Heat the oil in a large skillet over medium-high heat.
4. Meanwhile, if using, prepare the tempura batter according to the Instructions on the package.
5. Once the oil is hot, dip the pasta mixture into the tempura batter and carefully place in the hot oil. Fry until golden brown, about 3-4 minutes.
6. Remove the tempura carbonara from the oil and drain on a paper towel.
7. Serve the tempura carbonara with your favorite garnish such as chopped parsley and grated Parmesan cheese.

Nutrition Information:
Each serving of Carbonara Tempura provides approximately:
Calories: 500 | Total fat: 20g | Saturated fat: 7g | Cholesterol: 90mg | Sodium: 430mg | Total carbohydrates: 60g | Protein: 18g

85. Carbonara Scampi

Carbonara Scampi is an Italian-style seafood dish made with succulent shrimp and a creamy pasta sauce. It is quick to make and is incredibly flavorful, making it a great dish for a weeknight meal.
Serving: 4
Preparation Time: 15 minutes
Ready Time: 25 minutes

Ingredients:
- 2 tablespoons butter
- 1 or 2 cloves of garlic, minced

- 1/2 teaspoon paprika
- 1/4 teaspoon dried oregano
- 1 pound shrimp, peeled and deveined
- 2 tablespoons all-purpose flour
- 1/4 cup dry white wine
- 2 cups chicken broth
- 1/4 teaspoon freshly ground black pepper
- 1/4 teaspoon salt
- 2 tablespoons chopped fresh basil
- 4 ounces uncooked spaghetti
- 1/2 cup grated Parmesan cheese

Instructions:
1. Melt butter in a large skillet set over medium-high heat. Add garlic, paprika, and oregano and cook for 2 minutes.
2. Add shrimp and cook for 4 minutes. Remove from heat and set aside.
3. In the same skillet, melt butter over medium-high heat. Add flour and cook for 1 minute.
4. Add white wine, chicken broth, black pepper, and salt. Bring to a boil.
5. Reduce the heat to low and simmer for 5 minutes. Stir in the cooked shrimp.
6. Meanwhile, cook the spaghetti according to package Instructions. Drain the spaghetti and add to the skillet.
7. Stir in the Parmesan cheese and chopped fresh basil.
8. Serve immediately.

Nutrition Information:
Calories Per Serving: 305; Total Fat: 11.8g; Cholesterol: 180mg; Sodium: 890mg; Total Carbohydrates: 20.8g; Protein: 26.5g.

86. Carbonara Risotto

Carbonara Risotto is a flavorful mix of creamy rice and savory bacon flavors. Perfect for a cozy dinner or a meal-prep favorite, this risotto dish is incredibly easy to make and is sure to be a hit with the whole family.
Serving: 4
Preparation Time: 10 minutes
Ready Time: 25 minutes

Ingredients:
-4 slices bacon, diced
-1 onion, diced
-1 teaspoon minced garlic
-2 cups arborio rice
-6 cups chicken broth
-2 egg yolks
-½ cup grated parmesan cheese
-2 tablespoons cream
-2 tablespoons butter

Instructions:
1. Heat a large skillet over medium heat. Add bacon and sauté until slightly crispy, about 5 minutes. Add onion and garlic and sauté until the onion is tender and translucent, about 5 minutes.
2. Add rice and stir to coat in the bacon fat. Pour in 4 cups of the chicken broth and bring the mixture to a boil. Reduce heat to low and simmer until the rice has absorbed most of the liquid, about 10 minutes.
3. In a small bowl, whisk together the remaining 2 cups broth, egg yolks, parmesan cheese, cream and butter. Add to the rice and stir until combined. Continue stirring until the risotto is creamy and the cheese has melted.
4. Serve and enjoy!

Nutrition Information:
Calories: 470
Total Fat: 20g
Saturated Fat: 11g
Cholesterol: 128mg
Sodium: 240mg
Carbohydrates: 48g
Fiber: 2g
Protein: 15g

87. Carbonara Polenta

Carbonara Polenta is a delicious Italian dish made of ground polenta that is cooked in a creamy cheese sauce and garnished with bacon and onion. It is a quick and easy dish that is sure to be a crowd pleaser.
Serving: 6
Preparation Time: 10 minutes
Ready Time: 25 minutes

Ingredients:
-2 cups polenta
-2 cups chicken stock
-1 cup grated Parmesan cheese
-4 slices bacon, cooked and crumbled
-1/2 cup finely chopped onion
-3 tablespoons butter
-Salt and pepper, to taste

Instructions:
1. Bring chicken stock to a boil in a medium saucepan.
2. Stir in the polenta. Reduce heat to low and cook for 10 minutes, stirring occasionally.
3. Remove the saucepan from the heat and stir in the Parmesan cheese, bacon, onion, butter, and salt and pepper.
4. Serve the polenta warm.

Nutrition Information:
Serving size: 1/6 of the recipe
Calories: 318 calories
Total Fat: 15 grams
Cholesterol: 23 milligrams
Sodium: 499 milligrams
Total carbohydrates: 32 grams
Dietary Fiber: 2 grams
Protein: 10 grams

88. Carbonara Goulash

Carbonara Goulash is an Italian-style dish consisting of pasta, cream, bacon, onions, cheese, and tomato sauce. It is an easy, comforting dish that can take the place of dinner or a light snack.
Serving : 4
Preparation Time : 10 minutes
Ready Time : 40 minutes

Ingredients:
- 8 ounces dry macaroni noodles
- 4 tablespoons butter
- 2 tablespoons all-purpose flour
- 1 1/2 cups whole milk
- 2 cloves garlic, minced
- 1/4 teaspoon freshly ground black pepper
- 1 cup shredded Italian cheese blend
- 1 large tomato, diced
- 4 ounces cooked bacon, diced
- 2 tablespoons chopped fresh parsley

Instructions: :
1. Preheat the oven to 350 degrees F.
2. Bring a large pot of salted water to a boil and add macaroni noodles.
3. Cook for about 8 minutes, or until noodles are tender. Drain the noodles and set aside.
4. In a medium saucepan, melt butter over medium heat. Add flour and whisk to combine.
5. Slowly whisk in milk and simmer until sauce thickens, about 5 minutes.
6. Stir in garlic, black pepper, shredded cheese, tomato, bacon, and cooked noodles.
7. Pour the mixture into a 9x13 inch baking dish and sprinkle with chopped parsley.
8. Bake for 25 minutes, or until golden brown and bubbly.

Nutrition Information :
ServingSize : 1 cup
Calories : 380
Total Fat : 22gm
Cholesterol : 45mg
Sodium : 400mg

Carbohydrates : 29gm
Protein : 14gm

89. Carbonara Chili

Carbonara Chili is a delicious twist on the classic Italian Carbonara that pairs spicy chili peppers with rich cream sauce and crispy bacon. It is a quick and easy dish perfect for weeknight dinners.
Serving: 4-6
Preparation Time: 10 minutes
Ready Time: 20 minutes

Ingredients:
-4 ounces bacon, diced
-1 red chili pepper, seeded and diced
-2 cloves garlic, minced
-2 tablespoons all-purpose flour
-2 cups half and half cream
-1/2 cup chicken broth
-1 teaspoon Italian seasoning
-1/2 cup grated Parmesan cheese
-1/4 cup heavy cream
-4 ounces spaghetti noodles, cooked

Instructions:
1. In a large skillet over medium-high heat, cook bacon until crisp. Stir in chili pepper and garlic, and cook for 1 minute.
2. Add the flour and stir until combined. Gradually add the half and half and chicken broth and stir until thickened.
3. Stir in the Italian seasoning and Parmesan cheese. Reduce heat to low and simmer for 10 minutes, stirring occasionally.
4. Stir in the heavy cream and cooked noodles. Simmer for 5 minutes or until heated through.

Nutrition Information: Per Serving – Calories 394, Fat 23.3g, Carbohydrate 27.7g, Fiber 2.1g, Protein 17.4g

90. Carbonara Soup

Carbonara Soup is a creamy, comforting Italian soup that's perfect for a cold day or weeknight dinner. It combines classic carbonara flavors, including pancetta, egg, Parmesan cheese, and cream, in an easy-to-make soup.

Serving: 4

Preparation Time: 20 minutes

Ready Time: 40 minutes

Ingredients:

2 tablespoons olive oil

1/2 cup of diced pancetta (or bacon)

1 large onion, diced

4 cloves of garlic, chopped

4 cups chicken broth

1/2 cup of heavy cream

1/2 teaspoon ground black pepper

2 large eggs

3/4 cup grated Parmesan cheese

Instructions:

1. Begin by heating the olive oil in a large pot over medium-high heat. Add the pancetta and cook until crisp, about 5 minutes.

2. Next, add in the diced onion and garlic and cook for an additional 3 minutes, stirring occasionally.

3. Pour in the chicken broth and bring to a boil. Once boiling, reduce heat to low and let simmer for 15 minutes.

4. Remove the pot from the heat and stir in the cream and pepper.

5. In a medium bowl, whisk together the eggs and grated Parmesan cheese.

6. Drizzle the egg mixture slowly into the pot, stirring constantly. This should take about 1 minute.

7. Place the pot back over low heat and cook for an additional 3 minutes, stirring occasionally.

8. Serve and enjoy the Carbonara Soup!

Nutrition Information:

Calories: 345

Total Fat: 25.9g

Saturated Fat: 11.6g
Cholesterol: 115mg
Sodium: 1176mg
Carbohydrates: 8.2g
Fiber: 1.1g
Sugar: 3.3g
Protein: 16.3g

91. Carbonara Stew

Carbonara Stew is a rich and flavorful dish that combines many of the traditional flavors of an Italian Carbonara. It's made with bacon, cream, and cheese for a creamy, hearty, delicious stew that can be served on its own or as a side.
Serving: 4-6
Preparation Time: 10 minutes
Ready Time: 30 minutes

Ingredients:
- 8 slices bacon, diced
- 1 large onion, diced
- 4 cloves garlic, minced
- 2 1/2 cups chicken broth
- 1/2 cup heavy cream
- 1/2 cup Parmesan cheese, grated
- 1 teaspoon dried Italian herb blend
- 1/4 teaspoon black pepper
- 2 tablespoons olive oil
- 4 cups cooked egg noodles

Instructions:
1. In a large skillet over medium heat, cook the bacon until it is lightly browned and slightly crisp.
2. Add in the onion and garlic and saute for another 3 minutes, stirring frequently.
3. Pour in the chicken broth, cream, Parmesan cheese, and Italian herb blend and stir well.

4. Bring the mixture to a boil, reduce heat to low, and simmer for 15 minutes, stirring occasionally.

5. Heat olive oil in a separate skillet over medium-high heat. Once hot, add the cooked egg noodles and cook until lightly browned.

6. Add the cooked noodles to the skillet with the bacon mixture and stir to combine.

7. Simmer another 5 minutes to allow everything to combine and heat through.

Nutrition Information: (Per Serving)
Calories: 400 kcal
Protein: 16 g
Fat: 23 g
Carbohydrates: 23 g
Fiber: 1

92. Carbonara Broth

Carbonara Broth
Serving: 4
Preparation Time: 20 minutes
Ready Time: 40 minutes

Ingredients:
- 4 cups chicken broth
- 2 tablespoons butter
- 1 1/2 cups diced cooked bacon
- 1 cup diced onion
- 1/2 cup grated Parmesan cheese
- 2 tablespoons cornstarch
- 2 tablespoons all-purpose flour
- 1/2 teaspoon freshly ground black pepper
- 1/4 teaspoon garlic powder
- 2 cups heavy cream
- 2 tablespoons chopped fresh parsley

Instructions:
1. Heat the chicken broth in a large saucepan over medium heat.

2. In a separate large skillet, melt the butter over medium-high heat. Add the bacon and onion and sauté until the onion is translucent, about 5 minutes.
3. Add the Parmesan, cornstarch, flour, black pepper, and garlic powder to the onion and bacon mixture. Heat until the mixture thickens, stirring frequently, about 5 minutes.
4. Add the heavy cream to the onion and bacon mixture, stirring constantly until it thickens, about 10 minutes.
5. Pour the chicken broth and bacon mixture into the broth in the saucepan. Simmer for 15 minutes.
6. Garnish with parsley before serving.

Nutrition Information per Serving: Calories 425, Fat 32g, Sodium 631mg, Carbohydrates 14g, Fiber 1g, Protein 18g

93. Carbonara Gravy

Carbonara Gravy is a classic Italian dish made with bacon, grated cheese, egg, and black pepper. It's a creamy and delicious way to turn pasta into an unforgettable meal.
Serving: 4
Preparation Time: 15 minutes
Ready Time: 15 minutes

Ingredients:
- 6 slices thick-cut bacon, diced
- 4 cloves garlic, chopped
- 2 large egg yolks
- 1/2 cup grated parmesan cheese
- 1/4 teaspoon black pepper
- 1/2 cup heavy cream
- 2 tablespoons chopped fresh parsley
- 1 pound cooked pasta

Instructions:
1. In a large skillet, cook the bacon over medium heat until it begins to crisp, about 5 minutes.
2. Add the garlic and cook for 1 minute more.

3. Meanwhile, whisk together the egg yolks, cheese, and pepper in a small bowl.
4. Reduce the heat to low and add the cream to the skillet. Simmer until the sauce is slightly thickened, about 1 minute.
5. Add the egg yolk mixture to the skillet and stir until combined.
6. Add the cooked pasta to the skillet and toss to combine.
7. Add the parsley and stir to combine.

Nutrition Information (per serving): Calories: 480, Fat: 22g, Cholesterol: 135mg, Sodium: 533mg, Carbohydrates: 42g, Fiber: 2g, Protein: 21g.

94. Carbonara Sauce

Carbonara sauce is a creamy pasta dish that originated in Rome, Italy. It is typically served over pasta and features pancetta, eggs, and Parmesan cheese.
Serving: 4
Preparation time: 15 minutes
Ready time: 15 minutes

Ingredients:
- 1 tablespoon olive oil
- 4 ounces chopped pancetta
- 1 garlic clove, minced
- 3 large eggs
- 2/3 cup freshly grated Parmesan cheese
- 3/4 teaspoon freshly ground black pepper
- 1 pound cooked al dente spaghetti

Instructions:
1. Heat olive oil in a large saucepan over medium-high heat.
2. Add pancetta and garlic to the pan and cook until the pancetta is crisp, about 8 minutes.
3. In a separate bowl, whisk together the eggs, Parmesan cheese, and black pepper.
4. Add cooked spaghetti to the saucepan with the pancetta and garlic.

5. Pour the egg mixture over the spaghetti and stir until the eggs begin to thicken, about 2 minutes.
6. Serve warm and garnish with additional Parmesan cheese, if desired.

Nutrition Information:
Amount per serving: Calories: 413, Total Fat: 17.2 g, Saturated Fat: 6.5 g, Cholesterol: 147 mg, Sodium: 568 mg, Total Carbohydrate: 49.8 g, Dietary Fiber: 3.0 g, Protein: 16.8 g

95. Carbonara Dressing

Carbonara Dressing is a creamy Italian condiment that is perfect to top off a variety of dishes. It adds amazing flavor to pizzas, pastas, sandwiches, and more.
Serving: 8
Preparation time: 5 minutes
Ready time: 10 minutes

Ingredients:
- 2 tablespoons olive oil
- 1/4 cup fresh parsley
- 2 cloves of garlic, minced
- 1/3 cup Parmesan cheese, freshly grated
- 2 tablespoons lemon juice
- Salt and pepper to taste
- 1/2 cup mayonnaise

Instructions:
1. In a medium bowl, mix the olive oil, parsley, garlic, Parmesan, lemon juice, and salt and pepper to taste.
2. Stir in the mayonnaise until well combined.
3. Serve with your favorite meals.

Nutrition Information:
Per Serving: 140 calories, 14 g fat, 2 g carbohydrates, 4 g protein.

96. Carbonara Marinade

Carbonara Marinade is an easy and delicious marinade with a powerful combination of smoky bacon, creamy Parmesan, and a hint of garlic. The perfect dish for a special dinner or lunch, this marinade will elevate your meal with its bold flavor.

Serving: Serves up to 6
Preparation Time: 15 minutes
Ready Time: 45 minutes

Ingredients:
- ½ cup extra-virgin olive oil
- 2 cloves garlic, minced
- ½ teaspoon red pepper flakes
- 6 strips bacon, chopped
- 1/3 cup freshly grated Parmesan cheese
- ¼ teaspoon salt
- 2 tablespoons freshly chopped Italian parsley

Instructions:
1. In a medium bowl, combine olive oil, garlic, red pepper flakes, and bacon. Mix until the bacon is evenly coated.
2. Transfer the mixture to a large baking dish.
3. Bake in a preheated 375°F oven for 20 minutes, or until bacon is golden and crisp.
4. Remove from oven and sprinkle the Parmesan cheese, salt, and parsley over top.
5. Use the Carbonara Marinade immediately on your favorite proteins or vegetables.

Nutrition Information (per serving): Calories 330, Total Fat 29g, Saturated Fat 7g, Cholesterol 20mg, Sodium 380mg, Total Carbohydrate 6g, Dietary Fiber 3g, Protein 9g.

97. Carbonara Rub

Carbonara Rub is an Italian dish that is traditionally made with bacon, eggs, and cheese. The addition of spices makes this a warm and hearty dish that is full of flavor.

Serving: 4-6

Preparation Time: 10 minutes

Ready Time: 30-45 minutes

Ingredients:

- 4 slices of bacon
- 2 eggs
- 2 cups of freshly grated parmesan
- 2 tablespoons of Italian seasoning
- 1 teaspoon of black pepper
- Salt to taste

Instructions:

1. Preheat oven to 350F.
2. Grease a 9-inch baking dish with a non-stick cooking spray.
3. In a small skillet, cook bacon over medium heat until crisp. Drain bacon on a plate lined with paper towels.
4. In a medium bowl, beat eggs and add parmesan cheese. Mix in Italian seasoning, black pepper, and salt.
5. Cut bacon pieces into small pieces and add to the egg and cheese mixture.
6. Pour egg-bacon mixture into the prepared baking dish and bake in preheated oven for 30-45 minutes.
7. Serve warm and enjoy!

Nutrition Information:

Calories: 343, Total Fat: 24g, Saturated Fat: 10g, Cholesterol: 122mg, Sodium: 660mg, Total Carbohydrates: 2g, Sugar: 0g, Protein: 25g.

CONCLUSION

The Carbonara Cornucopia: 97 Delicious Variations of the Classic Pasta Dish is an inspiring cookbook that celebrates the sheer versatility of the beloved carbonara dish. It contains 97 creative and delicious variations of this classic pasta dish, with each recipe incorporating unique ingredients that take the dish to new heights.

This cookbook is a must-have for carbonara lovers everywhere, as it introduces them to a whole new world of flavors and textures, all while staying true to the essence of this beloved dish. From traditional carbonaras to innovative, unconventional twists, this cookbook has something for everyone.

One of the things that makes The Carbonara Cornucopia such a standout cookbook is its attention to detail. The recipes are easy to follow and have been thoughtfully crafted to ensure that each dish is as flavorful and satisfying as the last. Additionally, the introduction to each recipe offers tips and guidance on how to make the dish even more delicious – whether it's through ingredient substitutions or cooking techniques.

Another standout feature of this cookbook is its ability to showcase the versatility of carbonara. With close to a hundred different variations, one can't help but marvel at the endless possibilities that this dish offers. From adding vegetables, to using alternative proteins, to playing with spices and herbs – the sky is truly the limit with carbonara.

The Carbonara Cornucopia also stands out because of its sheer variety. Whether you're a vegetarian, a pescatarian, or a meat lover, there is a recipe in this cookbook that will meet your needs. It has sweet, savory, spicy, and mild dishes that are sure to satisfy any palate.

Moreover, this cookbook offers a great way to showcase one's culinary creativity. With such a versatile dish like carbonara, one can make a variety of unique dishes that are sure to impress family and friends. This cookbook is an excellent tool for taking the classic carbonara to new heights by experimenting with new ingredients.

In conclusion, The Carbonara Cornucopia: 97 Delicious Variations of the Classic Pasta Dish is a cookbook that should be in everyone's kitchen. It's a testament to the versatility of carbonara and an invitation to explore the many possibilities that this dish offers. Whether you are an experienced cook or just starting, this cookbook offers something for everyone. It's an amazing resource and a must-have for any carbonara lover, and its repertoire of recipes will keep one inspired for years to come.

Printed in Great Britain
by Amazon

32905700R00066